Lens of
an Infantryman

# Lens of an Infantryman

*A World War II Memoir
with Photographs
from a Hidden Camera*

MURRAY LEFF

McFarland & Company, Inc., Publishers

*Jefferson, North Carolina, and London*

LIBRARY OF CONGRESS CATALOGUING-IN-PUBLICATION DATA

Leff, Murray, 1922–
Lens of an infantryman : a World War II memoir with photographs
from a hidden camera / Murray Leff.
Includes index.
p.      cm.

ISBN-13: 978-0-7864-2867-0
softcover : 50# alkaline paper ∞

1. Leff, Murray, 1922–    2. World War, 1939–1945 — Photography.
3. World War, 1939–1945 — Personal narratives, American.    4. World
War, 1939–1945 — Campaigns — Western Front — Pictorial works.
5. United States. Army — Biography.    6. United States. Army. Infantry
Division, 35th.    7. War photography — Europe.    8. Soldiers —
United States — Biography.    I. Title.
D810.P4L44    2007        940.54'1273092 — dc22        2007013996
[B]

British Library cataloguing data are available

Cover photograph: Self portrait of Murray Leff, Co. E, 137th Infantry

Manufactured in the United States of America

*McFarland & Company, Inc., Publishers
Box 611, Jefferson, North Carolina 28640
www.mcfarlandpub.com*

# CONTENTS

# ACKNOWLEDGMENTS

To the guys who didn't make it back and especially to
"Kap" Keplinger who helped me dig my first foxhole —
and to Sgt. Rich with whom I shared many foxholes.
They were deprived of the full life I was able to enjoy.

With thanks to
Richard Klein, my son-in-law, who was my computer "guru."
Without him I would never have been able to put this memoir
on a disk ready for the publisher. In my desire to get this on paper
it was inevitable that there would be many grammatical errors,
omissions and other shortcomings. Mildred Schwartz, my
long-time friend and English expert, caught and corrected what I
overlooked. And, of course, my wife Selma, who put up with my
endless hours on the computer, and offered support even when
there were other things she would rather have done.

# INTRODUCTION

When World War II ended in August of 1945 my outfit, the 35th Infantry Division, was in the pipeline on the way from Europe to the United States. The original plan had called for us to have a thirty day furlough and then go on to the invasion of Japan.

It seems predetermined logistical arrangements could not be altered for our immediate discharge on reaching the United States. Instead we were given the thirty day furlough called for in the original plan. During those thirty days, as reality started catching up to those in charge, they kept extending the furlough until after seventy days they found a way to have us discharged.

It was during those seventy days that I scribbled down everything I could remember of the year before. At the end of the seventy days I had not yet finished. In fact I had only brought the story up to February 1945. It was then that I was ordered to Fort Dix to be discharged. Before I left for Fort Dix I put what I had done in an envelope, which I did not open again for fifty-seven years.

However, during the war, in March of 1945, I had gotten hold of a camera and started taking pictures. It is with the aid of these photographs that I was able to complete this narrative.

The above mentioned scribbling was not intended to be a piece of "literature." It was merely a simple, direct record of events in the jargon and foxhole grammar of that time and place. Nor is there any attempt to hide occasional incidents where the instinct for survival challenged the requirements of the mission. For me it is a piece of history of which I was personally a part. It is for the reader to find whatever subjective reactions come to him.

When Hitler was first coming to power around 1936, my brother and I were developing pictures in a converted clothes closet at home. I spent many happy days at the World's Fair of 1939 taking pictures I still look at. Going overseas I took a camera and film with me. Unfortunately (or perhaps fortunately) this camera disappeared along with a barracks bag I brought up to the Company E kitchen where it was supposed to await my return from the front line. It is possible that the loss of that camera saved my life. For me taking pictures in combat was a distraction from the unspeakable horrors which were so common then. At the same time this photography was also distracting me (at least somewhat) from keeping my head down when it was the thing to do.

And so I lived through the worst of my war in Northern France and the "Battle of the Bulge" without a camera. It was only when we reached Germany that I got one. I was able to trade my cigarette ration for a 35 MM folding bellows camera called "Welti." When it was folded closed in its case I was able to conceal it under my field jacket. I believe it had an f3.5 lens and a Compur shutter.

Unlike most cameras today, the exposure and distance had to be set manually. Winding the film was also manual. In addition, the films of that era were much less sensitive than those currently available. That meant setting the distance and shutter speed on the camera had to be more precise. Moreover, movement of the camera or the subject was more likely to result in a blurred or out of focus picture.

As a result of the above, a few of the photos that follow are not as precise as I could wish. Some of the conditions I encountered — inadequate light and movement by myself and the subject plus the distraction of incoming mail (German artillery)— made taking pictures in a combat situation quite challenging.

Getting film for the camera was not a big problem. When I could not buy the film I took a roll or two off the shelf of an abandoned, wrecked camera store. After Germany surrendered and we were on occupation duty, I was able to make a deal with a camera store to use their darkroom. It was at this point that I was able to develop the film and make some prints of the pictures that I had shot in combat.

Taking pictures in a combat zone was really against orders. Indeed, I was ordered not to do it. However, I had the feeling they simply meant I should not get caught doing it, especially by officers of another unit. With the war over, these same officers sought me out to take pictures of a big parade the 35th was staging in Brussels. They gave me a jeep and driver to take me to Brussels for the parade. Later the same jeep and driver took me to Antwerp where the Signal Corps had set up a darkroom. It was great! I was doing what I liked best and getting paid for it. Some of these pictures are in the regimental and division history books.

There is an unexplainable reward I get out of photography. It feels like magic to capture a moment in time and have it forever. More recently I have been trying to make pictures with an artistic quality. Not only should the picture be interesting; I also try to incorporate qualities of composition, color, texture, etc. Photography has fascinated me all my life and continues to do so.

# 1 | MY TRIP TO THE 35TH

September 10, 1944 — At around eleven o'clock in the morning, after being fed doughnuts and coffee by the Red Cross, we walked up the gang plank. A band was playing the latest swing numbers. The ship, called the *Mount Vernon*, was converted from the luxury liner U.S.S. *Washington*.

After getting our bunks assigned we came up on deck. Around three o'clock we began to move. Before dark the Port of Boston was lost in a glorious sunset.

For the most part the trip over was great. With the exception of one day there was nothing but blue skies and fluffy white clouds in the daytime and beautiful sunsets toward evening. Oh, for my camera! I had to turn it in during the trip and wasn't to get it back until we hit France. During the daylight hours I'd stretch out on the deck stripped to the waist to soak in the sun, all the while reading books that were distributed to us for the trip. We got a chance to buy candy and cigarettes. The cigarettes were 50 cents a carton. Later some of the boys sold them for ten dollars a carton to French railroad men near Paris. I used them in trade for French bread and cider.

Our morale got a boost with the three sound movies that were shown in a screened-in area of the deck. After the first night sleeping in my bunk I made the open deck my sleeping quarters. Right after supper I'd get my blankets and come up on deck. We would sit on the deck listening to the radio and watch the sun go down over the tail end of the ship.

At dusk the loudspeaker would blare out, "Throughout the ship, the smoking lamp is out." At that time the garbage detail would start heaving the garbage over the rear end of the ship. All during the day the garbage would accumulate on the aft deck but it would not be thrown overboard for fear of leaving a trail for submarines to follow. Another precaution against submarines was the changing of course every ten minutes or less. Owing to the speed of our converted luxury liner, we were able to travel alone without a convoy.

After darkness came and most of the boys had gone below, we spread our blankets on the deck and went to sleep. The next thing I knew, just before dawn, a bugle would be blown and we were all chased below, while the crew manned the ship's guns. The theory behind all this was that you can never tell what might be sitting around your part of the ocean when it gets light.

The morning of the 16th, as it got light, we discovered two British destroyers escorting us in. On the 17th we sighted land. In the afternoon we approached the harbor of Liverpool with its barrage balloons. About that time they made everyone go below. It wasn't until after we had docked that we were allowed up on deck again. We watched, waved and whistled as ferry boats came close by.

September 18, 1944 — It wasn't until two o'clock at night that we debarked. We walked through a couple of deserted Liverpool dock streets to a railroad station. After getting on the train we got our doughnuts and coffee from British Red Cross girls. We considered the British train slightly uncomfortable because of the hard seats — but it turned out to be the best train ride we had in the E.T.O. (European Theater of Operations).

I managed to get a few hours' sleep before I awoke to find it was raining. I opened my first K ration in Europe and had breakfast.

England seemed dirty and grimy. Later I found out this was due to the rationing of paint. I remember seeing lots of hedgerow country which might have looked very much nicer if it weren't so rainy and foggy. We passed through several towns and cities. The only ones I remember are Rugby and London. Many sections of London showed signs of being blitzed, but in general the damage seemed to be repaired in good time. We were supposed to be able to see the Houses of Parliament and I think I did catch a glimpse of them, but I am not sure. That afternoon we reached Southampton. We walked through part of the military port. I was impressed by the scale of things — row on row of assault boats, equipment and munitions.

We boarded a lend-lease Liberty ship manned by a British crew. About four o'clock the next morning the ship pulled out of Southampton. Around noon we dropped anchor off Omaha Beach. I saw troops debarking from another ship not far away. There was a large LST (Landing Ship Tank) alongside the troop ship. First the troops would throw their duffle bags over the side of the mother ship into the LST. Then they would follow the bags over the ship's side into the landing craft via a landing net.

We were lucky! We had small LCPs (Landing Craft Personnel) suspended from davits right at deck level. When our turn came we clambered into the LCP with our duffle bags. Then the whole landing craft was lifted up and over the side and lowered into the water. The trip to the shore was rather nice, especially since no one was shooting at us. We passed through a gap in a long line of sunken ships. At last our boat hit a small floating ramp and the front door was lowered. I grabbed my duffle bag and walked down over the door, which also served as a gang plank, on to the ramp. The ramp could not have been very buoyant because as I stepped on the ramp, it sank beneath the water and I got my feet wet.

We walked up the ramp on to the beach where our company was assembling. Here they gave us a chance to catch our breath. It was now that I was able to see what Omaha Beach was all about. It was situated in a cove with the neck of the cove sealed off from the North Sea by a long line of sunken ships. There were all kinds of ships, including destroyers, cargo ships and others. It seemed like there could have been a hundred of them. In the center of the line was a gap through which flowed a constant stream of small landing craft.

The beach itself was a scene of constant activity. Here and there were an occasional German pill box and pieces of German equipment. Up on the hill, to the right, was a gigantic American military cemetery. From the beach we moved off onto a long winding trail that led up a high cliff on to the flat hedgerow country of Normandy. We walked through a small battered village where I was immensely gratified by the fact that I could read and translate part of an old advertisement in French painted on the side of a building.

Passing many fields filled to capacity with row on row of tents we finally came to an empty pasture. Here we proceeded to "Form for shelter tents" so that we could pitch our tents in exactly straight lines. The insistence of the officer in charge that we do a perfect job disgusted me. It was quite apparent that some rear echelon commander was bucking for promotion and we who were going into combat had to pay for it. I'll bet he got a Bronze Star for Meritorious Service.

The fellow that I pitched my tent with had buddied up with me back in Ft. Meade from which we left for Boston, our Port of Embarkation. His name was Levoncheck. As we were constantly arranged alphabetically, he was right in back of me at all formations. He told a good story and I was a good listener so we hit it off first rate. He had a wife and two kids back in Pennsylvania.

The days were quite comfortable but the nights were cold so we liked to heat our rations instead of eating them cold. Unlike K rations where, for heat, you can burn the waxed box in which they come, the C rations we were given came in a tin can. And so we hunted for firewood in the hedgerows despite the warning that they had not yet been cleared of mines. At any rate, for the two days that we were there we had hot food.

Before dawn on the day we left they had us strike our tents and make up our packs in the dark. We policed the area while it started to get light and then formed up to get on trucks, rushing like hell all the while. It was two more hours before the trucks came and we were off on the famous "Red Ball Highway." This was a one way road marked by signs showing a large red ball.

We passed St. Lo, which was really flattened. It was here that my future outfit had its first big fight. Next came Vire, which was also in a bad state. It looked like everything had gone through a meat grinder. The only thing of value was the road that had been cleared right through the middle of this desert of wrecked buildings. In the whole mess there wasn't one building left untouched. Occasionally an entire section of a house would be left standing. These reminded me of doll houses that come apart so that you can see the interior, much as you might see it in a legitimate stage play.

The people of France knew there was a war going on. And they knew who was fighting it for them. Everywhere we went they waved to us and made "V" for Victory signs with their fingers. They threw fruit to us whenever they had some. We would throw parts of our rations back to them. Although many French children waved to us for candy, I felt most of the French people were genuinely glad to see us.

The next towns I remember are Flers, Argentan and finally Le Mans. Le Mans was in pretty good shape and the population gave us a royal welcome as we roared through the streets. Thirteen miles south of Le Mans was our destination, another Replacement Depot. Here we pitched our tents in a little more irregular fashion. I had expected to get more training before we hit the front, and this is where we got some. From the way this training was conducted, I had the feeling it was mostly to keep us busy while waiting for our next move. We had two conditioning hikes and demonstrations of enemy equipment. I even got to throw a live German potato masher grenade. It was here we also got rid of our anti-gas impregnated uniforms that we had dragged all the way from the United States.

It was here that, for the first time, I engaged in a conversation with a French boy of fifteen who was studying English. Here too I managed to trade some bars of soap for a loaf of bread and two bottles of cider. One night after we had gone to bed, they got us all up to draw rifles. After standing around for an hour I finally got my rifle. It had been used quite a bit so all the working parts moved easily. I was pleased with it. After drawing the rifle I went back to bed. A couple of hours later they woke everybody up again to draw a rifle tool. That was just too much. I did not get up to get one. The next day there was time to issue rifles five times before we went to the range to zero them in.

About four days later we were told to get ready to move out. Early in the morning we boarded trucks and were driven to a small railroad station nearby. We got there around eight o'clock and sat down to wait for a train. A local merchant brought cases of wine and cognac for us. I managed to get one shot before it was all gone.

I found out from a Frenchman who seemed to know, that there was no train scheduled until noon. On hearing this Levoncheck and I took off to see what we could see. We slipped by the M.P.s (military police) and got into the center of town. As we passed one house an elderly couple beckoned to us. They filled our helmets with apples, peaches and grapes. We then drank to each other's health with wine and cognac.

We boarded the train a little after noon. We got a small, open gondola car with the floor space of the regular forty and eights but without the roof of the "quarante hommes ou huit cheveaux." How the French got forty men into one of these cars is beyond me. We had thirty-four men with equipment and rations for three days, and we could hardly move. Just as we pulled out, one of the guys sitting on the rear edge of the car fell off because of the sudden start. We picked him up with a cracked skull.

It seemed for every a mile or two the train would go forward, we would have to back up three or four miles. Soon it started to get dark and everybody settled down to get some sleep. Levoncheck and I huddled together on our duffle bags with our backs against the side of the car. I threw my overcoat over my head for warmth and tried to sleep.

When it got light again the train stopped for about an hour, at which time we got off and heated our rations. We used the wood ration boxes as a source of heat. After I finished, a Frenchman and his son came rushing down with a coffee pot full of hot water. He offered it to us to make coffee or hot chocolate. I gave him a cigarette and a "merci, monsieur." The kid then gave me a tomato. The engineer tooted his whistle. We climbed aboard and we were off again. We stopped for a short time in a small town where I traded a pack of cigarettes for a loaf of bread. For lunch that day I had a gigantic sandwich of French bread and tomatoes.

The train passed within twenty miles of Paris. The Eiffel Tower was visible in the far distance. We passed by the pockmarked battlefields of the previous war, the Argonne Forest and Verdun. We stopped for a while in the town of Verdun. Although it wasn't badly torn up, it seemed deserted. It was in Verdun, for the first time, that I saw the FFI or Forces Francaise de l'Interior. This tough looking civilian was working on his car. On both the arm band he wore and on his car were printed the three letters, FFI. These Frenchmen had been fighting the Germans all during the occupation. Inside the car on the seat was a "grease gun," a cheap type of American submachine gun.

Three days and two nights out of Le Mans we arrived at our destination, less than three hundred miles away. It was another Replacement Depot. This one was fifteen miles away from Metz, which was still in German hands. At night we could see the flashes and hear the rumbling of our artillery. The mud there was pervasive. Levoncheck and I looked for the highest spot we could find and pitched our tent there. We were offered more clothes should we want them. I picked up four handkerchiefs.

Two days later we boarded trucks again and were on our way. We had about an eight hour ride parallel to the front headed south to the next Replacement Depot. Arriving after dark, Levoncheck and I pitched our tent and went to sleep. I got up the next morning and went to the hot chow in the rain. The food was really very good. After I finished eating I went to throw the remnants of my meal into a garbage can.

There in front of the garbage cans stood several children, ankle deep in mud, holding cans and pails. They were begging for scraps. I took several pictures with my camera. I remember one shot I took of a small girl with a red rain cape holding a pail. She was standing there in the rain. Over her head nailed to a tree was a sign which read, "EVERYBODY SALUTES IN PATTON'S ARMY." About a mile away could be seen the three communities that make up the city of Nancy.

We were not to sleep at that depot even another night. That afternoon we were assigned to the 35th Infantry Division, loaded on trucks and driven down to Division Headquarters in Nancy.

# 2 | GREMERCEY FOREST

Thirty-fifth Division Headquarters was in a chateau near the main square of Nancy. In the courtyard in front of 35th headquarters I heard them assign me to the 137th Regiment. Levoncheck and Radioli were assigned to the 320th Regiment. I knew Radioli way back in school in the R.O.T.C. Just as it got dark the regimental trucks came for us and we said good-bye. I didn't see Radioli again until after V-E Day in Camp Lucky Strike when we were about to embark for home. Radioli was in a battalion headquarters company and a staff sergeant. At Camp Lucky Strike, he told me Levoncheck had been assigned to a rifle company and had been killed.

We got to regimental headquarters after dark, pitched tents and went to sleep. The next morning we were assigned to companies. I was to be in "Easy" Company along with two other fellows that I had become acquainted with in Ft. Meade.

We were led to our company kitchen, which was not very far away. There we got a breakfast of especially good hot cakes. We always had a good kitchen force. "Chung" Hill was the mess sergeant. I was told he had been a cook in the 35th Division in World War I. I was also told he had one brother in the weapons platoon of our company and another brother fighting close by. It seems he was sent home with a nervous breakdown after learning both brothers were killed.

After going through the chow line for seconds we turned in our mess kits. They told us we would not need them anymore. Next, they took us into a tool house where they put us into "fighting shape." Most of the boys had thrown away their barracks bags, while I still had mine in my pack. Everyone without a barracks bag would have to throw away what he would not carry anymore. I put my camera, eyeglasses, etc. into my barracks bag. I was told the kitchen would take care of it for me while I was on the line. I never saw my barracks bag again. We were told to put on our cleanest and best underwear, shoes, leggings, etc. Our packs would hold only rations, toothbrush, soap, razor, stationery and one blanket. We made a bed roll out of the other blanket and shelter half. I was going to carry my overcoat under my arm. I had stuffed a change of underwear and socks into the pockets of the coat.

After getting ready, I got a chance to write a letter home dated October 1, 1944. My new permanent address was Co.E, 137 Inf. APO 35 c/o P.M. New York, N.Y. Before noon we got on trucks and were taken to the supply sergeant's establishment in the village of Gremercey. There we got all the ammunition we wanted. I took three bandoliers and two grenades. While we were getting ammunition we got some incoming mail (a German artillery barrage). We all dropped to the floor but I wasn't as frightened as I expected to be. I said as much to the guy giving out the ammo. He told me that one of our boys had been killed in the next house only the day before by just such a barrage. I changed my attitude.

Shortly after noon ten of us piled on two jeeps and took off for Battalion Headquarters. We were warned that we would have to jump off as soon as we stopped because the enemy could see us and they would shell a halted vehicle. Going up that road I saw my first dead German. He was lying on his back as if he were lying in state. His helmet was still on and he wore a long overcoat. It seemed like a dream. As the jeeps stopped we all jumped out. Battalion Headquarters was at the top of a long hill in a wrecked white chateau. We got up there and flopped down to rest. In the garden of the chateau lay the body of an American artillery forward observer. I decided I would look the other way. One of his arms was blown off.

Soon a guide showed up to take us to the company CP (command post). We were asked to carry five gallon cans of water up to the line. This did not allow us to bring our overcoats as well. The guide took them from us and put them in the Battalion Headquarters, saying that we would get them later. I never saw mine again. We teamed up: one man would carry the two rifles and two bed rolls while the other man carried the water. It seemed like we must have gone several miles that way. I got so tired that once, coming on a dead German on the trail, I stepped over him rather than going around him.

Finally in mid afternoon we got to the company CP. Here "Topper" (First Sergeant Koch) told us the score and assigned us to platoons. The "score" was that an entire platoon had been captured two days before. Heady and I were assigned to the First Platoon. All in all there were ten of us that reported to the company that day. Out of the ten I believe I was the only one of a few not to get hit, killed or captured.

Captain Huff, the company commander, then crawled out of his hole to welcome us. He was bearded and gaunt. The day before, he explained, Lt. Azbell and he had spent eight hours playing dead in front of a German machine gun. In a little while Sgt. Watson, the platoon sergeant of the First Platoon, showed up. He wore a German pistol on his belt and a scarf around his neck. He had a hole in his helmet where some shrapnel or a bullet had gone through. He assigned Heady and me to the First Squad and then sent us to where they were dug in.

Once there we met Sgt. Rich, the squad leader. I remember him getting out of his hole and looking at us with his very large eyes. He took us over to a weak spot in the line and told us to dig in. The type of foxhole they were using was entirely unknown to me. If it hadn't been for "Kap" Keplinger showing us what to do and helping us we would not have had even this sloppy hole. However, it would have to do for our first night on the line. The unique feature of these holes was the top which protected you from "tree bursts" coming in from above.

The first night was a little frightening but not as bad as I expected. About three o'clock I was awakened to go on guard. Archie Campbell and I were sent out about fifty yards in front of the line into "No Man's Land" to act as a listening post. Naturally I was jumpy but what was bothering me most was the realization that I might have to actually kill another human being at any moment. I was brought up to feel that human life was sacred. After a couple of weeks of unremitting fear and misery my attitude changed. Moreover, this situation was brought about by an aggressive enemy with clearly evil goals. He had to be stopped.

Nor had I ever seen any dead people before that day. My emotions were in turmoil. After our turn on guard we went back to our respective holes and went to sleep. Hardly had I dozed off when we were awakened again for dawn alert. This alert required that everybody be awake for one hour before and after dawn.

The first thing we learned that morning was the best method of preparing a K ration meal. First, we filled the canteen cup half full with water. Then, after opening the can of meat about one quarter of the way with the key, we hooked said key over the lip of the cup. The next step was to prepare the wax container of the ration box to burn. We made two holes near the unopened end of the box and stood it on end. Lighting the opened end of the box had it burning like a candle. We then simply held the canteen cup with the can of meat over the fire until both were very hot. Finally, we dissolved the powdered coffee in the hot water, opened the can all the way and ate. Thus for breakfast we could have hot ham and eggs with biscuits and coffee. Afterwards there were fruit bars, cigarettes and chewing gum.

Our next job was to rebuild our hole. There had been shells falling during the night and the trees all around us were marked by shrapnel. First we dug a rectangular hole about six by four feet and about four feet deep. At one end of the hole a small sump is dug to collect water that leaks in. The sump makes it easier to bail out water. Next a cover for the hole is made by laying logs, branches, twigs, etc. over about three quarters of the hole. The opening is left at the sump end. Now we packed six or more inches of dirt on top. While shrapnel from a tree burst can still come through, we hoped it would be slowed enough to reduce the risk.

We started digging a narrow shallow hole quickly to use for some protection while working. Later the hole was widened and improved. When everything else was done, a shelter half was spread on the floor of the hole as a ground cover with blankets on top of the shelter half. A good two man hole could take all day to build.

On my second day on the line, Sweeny (Orville Swenson), a man who had been hit twice before, came back from the hospital. He had been a very good man until he was hit. Now his face turned white and he started to tremble when we had incoming mail. Because he was an old man, Rich told him to get into our hole with Heady and me. Ours was only a two man hole so we had to dig out the sides so that the three of us could fit into it.

On the third day they started bringing up "hot chow." Only one half of us could eat at one time; the other half would remain in or near their holes. The first group had the advantage in that they could eat from clean mess kits that had just been brought up to us. Also the food was a little warmer. After the first half had eaten they would return to their holes to relieve the second half and give them their dirty mess kits. Although the second half had to eat from dirty mess kits, they had the benefit of more leisure and the possibility of going back for seconds after everybody had eaten.

Toward late afternoon we were relieved and the entire company went back seven miles to the village of Gremercey. It was after dark when I finally stumbled into a bare room strewn with straw. I immediately made my bed and went to sleep. The next morning we got up a feast of "10 in 1" rations. This is a large carton filled with a large variety of food sufficient to feed ten men. By dinner time we had located a store of cherry, plum, peach and other preserves. In addition we got a frying pan, pots, pudding powder, grease and some milk from a nearby cow. "Kap" was our chief chef. He was always puttering around making something to eat. If we found a chicken it would not be long before we had southern fried chicken, that is if we could find the flour. It was not very long before many of the guys had the G.I.s (diarrhea).

It was during this stay in Gremercey that I found out who was in the First Squad. There was Sgt. Rich, the squad leader; Lux, first scout; Petrie, second scout;

Joe Jacobson the B.A.R. (Browning Automatic Rifle) man, and Lucas, his assistant. Heady and I made up one rifle team. Willie Zinnani and Archie Campbell made up the bazooka team. Another rifle team was made up of Keplinger and Phipps, who was second in command. A rifleman named Matt was transferred to another company. Another fellow whose nerve had cracked was transferred to the Anti-Tank Company.

We were only back a couple of days when we got orders to go out again. This new setup wasn't so bad because we were holding a secondary line. We didn't have to be so very careful because we knew there was another line between the Germans and us. There were holes already dug for us. All we had to do was spread our blankets and go to sleep. A jeep was almost able to get right up to us so we had hot food.

Phipps, the second in command, and I took one hole. We went to bed and were soon asleep. Towards four o'clock I felt a peculiar sensation on the side of my body. I was too sleepy to figure it out until later, when I accidentally touched the floor with my hand. I felt water. It had been raining and there were about two inches of cold, muddy water on the floor. I changed my position to get on a bump on the floor. That way I kept most of myself out of the water. Phipps woke up a little while later cursing like mad. He took a blanket from on top of us and put it under him.

After it got light we came out of our hole and pitched a tent on some high ground right near our hole. We crawled into it and tried to dry out a bit. Outside a cold wind was blowing. After a while we got some incoming mail. I suggested we get back in our hole while the shells were falling. "No!" said Phipps. He was too comfortable. He would not even put on his helmet. He had come to the outfit the same time I did but he came with a corporal's stripes, so he hated to take suggestions from anyone without stripes. In general he was a little pig-headed. He used to carry his grenades suspended by their safety rings from his harness. If one of the grenades had gotten tangled in the underbrush, he could have killed himself and anyone near him.

We were in the Gremercey Forest only a few days when we went back again to the village of Gremercey for a week in reserve. That week was quite pleasant. We slept in houses on straw. The kitchen stoves were brought up so that we could wait in line to get hot cakes right off the griddle. Once I went through the line four times, getting two cakes each time. We saw sound movies in a big barn. Because the floor was on an incline, you could lie on your back and watch the show.

I even got a chance to take a bath! I got a pass to the city of Nancy. My first stop was "Les Bains" or public bath house. At the entrance I bought a ticket and was given a box of bath salts. Later a woman attendant led me to a spacious bathroom

15

where she took the salts and dumped them into the bathtub while it was being filled with hot water. The first thing I did was shave with the first hot water since I left the U.S. Next I sank luxuriously into the hot salt water and just soaked for a while. It was an unbelievably great sensation.

It couldn't last forever. One evening Lt. Tompkins, the platoon leader, sent for all the squad leaders. In an hour Sgt. Rich came back with the "Big Picture" We were going to relieve some other outfit on the line. We would have six man outposts. Our outpost would have a .50 caliber machine gun. Each outpost had a telephone connected to higher headquarters in the rear.

We moved to our positions the next morning. When we got there we found one two-man hole and one three-man hole. Heady and Lux decided to dig their own hole in order to make everyone comfortable. The other holes were nothing more than portions of dried up stream beds with covers and a mound of earth on one end. Sgt. Rich and Sweeney took the larger hole upstream. Kibbler, who was in the Second Squad but attached to us for this job, was in the other hole with me.

With six men in one outpost we had a comparatively easy time. When things were quiet we could stand guard one hour and be off for five hours. Whenever things were stirring, two men would go on for two hours and be off for four. One of the good things about Rich was that he would always stand his share of guard although he was a staff sergeant and in command.

One rainy night Sgt. Rich stepped into my hole, woke me up, told me his hole was full of water and asked whether he could spend the night with us. He crawled in easily because Kibbler was then on guard. However, Kibbler was soon off guard so we ended up with three men in a two-man hole. After about an hour I heard a trickling noise but I didn't pay attention to it. Soon I felt water soaking through my clothes. As I started to get up I heard a big splash as a section of Rich's hole upstream gave way. In an instant our hole was a foot deep in water. We didn't waste time getting out. I managed to keep one of my blankets reasonably dry, but I was thoroughly wet on one side. It wasn't five minutes before the entire hole was full to the brim.

It was soon to become light so we all just stood around shivering in the cold rain. My blanket helped a little but it was soon soaked. After what seemed a long time it started to get grey and I could begin to make out shapes further and further away. The only way I had of telling whether these shapes were trees or Germans was to see if they moved. To be as inconspicuous as possible myself, I leaned against a broad tree. In due time the shapes became trees and I put my rifle down.

When it got light enough so that a fire would not be noticed, we cooked our breakfast with the "10 in 1" rations. After breakfast Kibbler and I decided to build a real hole. We picked a rise of ground about five feet higher than our previous position. At first we dug a deep narrow hole for safety while digging. Sure enough while we were digging we had some incoming mail and were indeed very lucky to have the protection of that small temporary hole.

We were fortunate in having the use of a full size axe so that we cut down several tall trees averaging about five inches in diameter. One man cut while the other widened the hole. We couldn't cut trees too near the edge of the forest because some German artillery observer might see the top of a tree shaking and send us some mail. We cut the logs to six feet in length and brought them back to the hole. There we arranged them to form a roof over the hole. On top of the logs we piled the earth we had excavated. Over this we laid our pup tent so that the rain would not penetrate. Over these shelter halves we threw stacks of autumn leaves for camouflage. It was so effective you couldn't see it from more than ten feet away. It was the best hole we ever made or saw.

One night while I was on guard one of our booby trap flares went off about three hundred yards in front of me. That meant there was something out there, possibly a German patrol or maybe only a cow. Immediately I whistled into the field phone and raised the platoon leader. (Whistling took the place of a bell. At night sound was a major concern in revealing your position.) I asked him to have a mortar barrage put down out there. For five minutes he tried to contact the mortars via the field phone. Meantime the outpost to my right, which belonged to the 320th Regiment, called me to ask if I had seen the flare. I told him I had and I was trying to get the mortars on it. He told me he could raise some fire from their Canon Company but that it was dangerous for them in that the flat trajectory shell of the cannon would skim over the trees with the possibility of hitting them and exploding over our own people.

The platoon leader finally called back and asked me if I thought the Germans were crawling up on me. I told him for all I knew that might be the case. He made the decision that all the automatic weapons of the platoon would open up at once. This didn't sound very good to me. Automatic weapons are prime artillery targets and I was standing behind a .50 caliber machine gun. I gave him my opinion and he hesitated. The lieutenant of a neighboring platoon heard our conversation and put his two cents in. He sided with me so we did not fire. We just waited for the Germans to come. The 320th outpost called and said they had decided not to use cannon fire but that they were alert and waiting.

In another hour it would be light. Rich decided to stay out in the outpost with me until after daybreak. A short time later Rich poked me and pointed to a shadowy figure on the horizon. I took the tape off the safety pin of one of my grenades and stared hard. Sure enough it seemed to move slightly, but we held our fire. It did seem peculiar, however, when after a half an hour that shadowy figure remained in the same general area. When it finally got light enough to see we both had a good laugh. The shadowy figure was the top of a fence post. The booby trap flare was set off by a German patrol. The flare frightened them away.

Another night while on guard I heard a rustling in the underbrush not very far away. Off came the tape from my grenade. I waited, literally, with bated breath. I held my breath so that I could hear better. For me the silence was so intense that I felt I could cut it with a knife. I had a finger through the ring of the grenade. There! I heard it again. I was so frightened I didn't have to make a conscious effort to keep from breathing. All of a sudden there was a great agitation in the underbrush and there in front of me ran a large field mouse.

Around November 3rd, we moved out toward a defensive position on the side of a bare hill in plain view of the enemy. We were supposed to get there a little after dark so that the Germans couldn't see us as we relieved the outfit was holding that position. Sgt. Rich, however, was in a rush so we got there ahead of schedule.

There was still some light when we walked out of the shelter of Gremercey Forest on to that open hillside. We had gone quite a distance when, without warning, I saw and heard a string of white tracers cut across in front of us. The next thing I knew I was on the ground trying to bury my head in the earth underneath my helmet. This was the first time anybody had specifically tried to kill me. There was a German on the opposite hill with a machine gun who was doing his darndest to get me and the others. Again and again he fired bursts at us.

Some bullets hit between me and the fellow in front. I could see the dirt flying. Maybe it got too dark or maybe he thought he got us all because after a while he stopped firing. We then called out to each other to see who was hit. Everybody was okay. When it was almost dark we got up and finally got to our holes.

Joe Jacobson, who had become my partner, and I got into this hole which was a pretty sad affair. It was too shallow and there was mud on the bottom. Moreover, it wasn't long enough for Joe who was about six feet tall. At Joe's suggestion we raised the cover a little. We then scraped the mud from the floor. We had found a German canteen cup and by digging the sump a little deeper we could use the cup to bail out the water that collected on the floor.

We also decided to enlarge the hole so Joe could stretch out. Joe did most of the work so later when it came time for me to wake him up for his hour of guard duty I stood it for him and then woke up the next guy. It was still difficult for Joe to stretch out so when we were both able to sleep I got into one corner and Joe curled around me.

During the day we had nothing to do but eat, sleep, write letters and relax in general. During daylight hours it was impossible to raise your head above the rim of the hole without being shot at by the machine gun on the next hill. The other main inconvenience was the lack of plumbing. The sump had to be bailed constantly. It being pretty cold we couldn't help urinating. We solved our dilemma by using the German canteen cup, the contents of which we could heave out of the hole without exposing ourselves. At night we could leave the hole and there was no such inconvenience.

With this enforced isolation, we began to discuss our situation and why we were in it. It seemed to me that if France and England had jumped on Hitler when he remilitarized the Rhineland in 1936, we would not be in this hole with a German machine gun shooting at us if we poked our heads up.

On about November 4th, after two solid days in this hole, we were relieved and moved back for a day of rest. We got back into Gremercey about two hours after dark and took over the cellar of a wrecked house. Immediately I staked my claim for a section of torn, worn and filthy mattress. Luckily one of the guys had a can of louse powder so that I was able to put a fine coat of white powder over the whole mattress. After spreading my blankets and eating I got ready for bed. Just about that time, Lafferty, the platoon runner, came in with the good news that there was going to be a night patrol and I was on it.

I was to be down at the company CP in five minutes with a stripped cartridge belt with the exception of a canteen. I wasn't to take any ammunition, rifle, shovel or identifying papers. In spite of this I kept my wallet in case I was captured. The CP was in a house that was slightly better preserved than our own. It was illuminated by a single headlight running on the current of a wire that ran to a jeep parked outside. The headlight was pointed upward toward the ceiling so that we got indirect light.

We were given "grease guns," cheap American submachine guns, and told how to operate them. I had never used one before but it was a very simple gun to operate and I had no trouble. We also got three magazines, each loaded with thirty .45 caliber cartridges. One magazine I put in the gun, and one in each breast pocket of my field jacket.

It was to be a ten man patrol. On a map they showed us where we were to go. We were supposed to follow a road until we came to a bridge. Having crossed the bridge, we were to make our way through the German lines to a certain road at one end of which was a German chow wagon. We were to have five men hidden on each side of the road. The idea was to ambush and capture any stray German that happened along the road.

There was a sergeant, Sgt. Cooper, who would go with us. He knew a little German and taught us a few expressions: "Hende Hoch!" means "Hands up"; "Nicht Shissen!" means "Don't shoot"; "Kommen sie hier!" means "Come here!" We were given our positions in the formation and our duties. "Blackie" Lincolnfelt and I were the connecting file between the two scouts up front and the main body behind us. Our job was to maintain contact between the scouts and the rest of the patrol. We were given cough drops in case we thought we might cough.

Two sergeants from G Company who supposedly had gone on similar patrols came in. They were to guide our patrol. They immediately appointed themselves the rear guard. Lt. Tompkins, my platoon leader, was in command but he wouldn't make a move without Sgt. Cooper.

We formed up on the road about nine o'clock and moved off. After a mile or two we came to our lines. We slipped through our wire and through one of our mine fields. The mines were laid in a regular pattern and were easy to avoid. There were five of us on each side of the road walking as noiselessly as possible. Every once in a while we would stop, lie down and listen. Right after we crossed our wire we found out the two G Company sergeants were missing. In the dark I nearly fell over a dead German in a ditch. As we approached the bridge we became more cautious, crouching close to the shoulder of the road and the ditch alongside.

We were about one hundred yards from the bridge when, without warning, a loud voice not very far ahead called out, "Stick Up! Stick Up!" In the moment that followed I was off the road and into the ditch. I was hardly down when a burst of machine gun fire came down the road. Then quiet, then another burst of fire followed by the explosion of a grenade about fifty feet from me. By that time I was well into the ditch. Not having any orders I just stayed there. Another grenade exploded in the same place.

Now we started to move back, keeping well down in the ditch. After possibly one hundred yards we stopped to see if everybody was there. Two guys, Murphy and Ortiz, weren't. After five or ten minutes I began to think they were hit. After about twenty minutes, when I was sure they were hit, they finally showed up. They had retreated a little more cautiously than the rest of us. Ortiz, a stocky Mexican, had a reputation as a "Kraut Killer." He was the only one carrying a Thompson submachine gun.

I had a real feeling of relief when we finally recrossed our barbed wire. Hiking back to the CP, we all felt we had done as good a job as could be expected and that it was a miracle no one got hit. At the CP they had hot coffee waiting for us. We drank the coffee while waiting for the report to be made. We turned in our grease guns and got ready to go home to bed. I stripped the top cartridge out of the magazine that I had carried in the gun. Not having to fire it, I considered it lucky.

We were about to leave when Capt. Huff, who was speaking to the colonel on the phone, motioned for us to come back. The colonel, it seems, had insisted we get a prisoner. After all, he felt, we were better off now that we knew the exact location of the German machine gun so we could go around it. We might even capture the German machine gunner from behind. It was a very discouraged group of G.I.s that filed out of the CP. I had now discarded my belt with the canteen. I just took the first aid pouch and replaced my lucky cartridge on top of the magazine that I put in the gun.

Off we went again. Just short of our wire we stopped to talk it over. According to Lt. Tompkins, the reason they wanted the prisoner was to find out what German unit we were facing. If we happened to kill our intended prisoner we were to take all his papers from him. I made the suggestion we go back and search the dead German I had tripped over in the ditch. This we did with no results. He had evidently already been searched.

Lt. Tompkins then led us diagonally across "no man's land" toward several hedgerows that we searched. We were hoping to set up an advanced listening or observation post. After we searched the third one, we dared go no further because the moon had come out. We set up a perimeter defense of the small woods and waited. It was then about one or two o'clock and a white frost started to settle on the grass. I hadn't worn my sweater so that I could move faster. We waited, watched and listened and got colder and colder.

The lieutenant didn't want to go back too soon because they might send us out again if there were enough darkness left. I knew that, so I didn't mind staying. Time after time I surely thought we had spent four or five hours there and it was only a matter of minutes before daylight came. Finally we got together and started home. This time there was no hot coffee waiting. Everyone in the CP had gone to sleep. Again I stripped my lucky cartridge from the top of the magazine. It had already worked twice. I hadn't had to fire it. (I still have that .45 caliber cartridge somewhere in my attic.)

On November 5th, I awoke around noon. That night we went out to some other exposed holes. It was about the same situation as the previous defensive position. It was here I celebrated my twenty-second birthday on November 6th, 1944.

# 3 | NOVEMBER 8, 1944

Towards evening of November 7th, Sgt. Rich came over to our hole. His face was white. "I've got some bad news for you, boys," he said. "We're jumping off in the morning!" I didn't know whether to believe him or not because he was always joking around. A little while later our relief came up and we went back to our cellar home.

We knew something was up when our platoon leader, Lt. Tompkins, was called to the company CP. Not much later, Tompkins called all the squad leaders together and gave them the "big picture." Finally Rich got our squad together and told us the story.

This was to be another D Day. There was to be a coordinated attack all along the front. Even the Russians were going to start an attack on the Eastern Front. Once we got going we might not stop until we reached Berlin.

The artillery was to start a terrific barrage at about four o'clock and stop at about six o'clock. The mortars were going to fire three hundred rounds just in the area that we would go through. We would start our attack right after the artillery lifted their barrage.

The company's mission was to take the village of Malaucourt. The mission of the First Platoon was to take the houses on the left side of the main street that ran through the middle of the village. The First and Second Squads were to be in the lead with the Third Squad in reserve. We could expect to get our feet wet because we had to cross a stream that was eighteen inches deep.

There were several things we would have to do before we could go to bed. We had to turn in our packs, draw ammunition and rations and make sure our weapons were working okay. We would have to be on the road ready to move at 4:15, so we decided we would get up at 3:45 in order to heat and eat our breakfast. In addition, some of us were to stand local security guard that night. Everybody agreed that was a dirty deal. It would be eleven o'clock before we could go to bed. This would leave us less than five hours' sleep.

Rich exploded. "To hell with it! Go to bed and forget about it!" Then he said, "If you're gonna do any praying, now's the time! We all might not be here tomorrow!" Some of the boys read Bibles. Lux was a Catholic so he had his rosary. We were all pretty quiet. I looked over the pictures of my family that I had in my wallet. We were really sweating it out.

As part of General Patton's Third Army our division, the 35th, raced across France until around October. They had to stop because of the difficulty in getting gasoline and other supplies up to the leading elements over such long distances in such a short time. While we were stopped, the Germans had time to harden their positions and make other plans to meet the attack they knew was coming. We all knew this and weren't happy about now having to break through these hardened defenses.

As promised, the artillery opened up all over, all at once. This was to be the first major attack for many of the boys, including myself. Then it came — the order to "get them on!" The platoon filed out on to the road and got into formation. The artillery was really crashing away. It was raining lightly when, in the darkness, the man in front of me turned around and said, "Heads up, we're moving out!" I followed him at the prescribed distance. Everybody had his own thoughts, but we all had the same mission. It took about an hour to get to our jumping off point. We lay down on the side of a hill and watched the artillery blast the Germans. There was hardly an instant when there wasn't a flash of light on the horizon, like rain drops hitting the pavement during a rain storm! The whistling of shells going over our heads was continuous.

Soon it started to get light. When the artillery barrage let up we knew we would be moving soon. Sure enough I saw Joe in front of me get up and start off. I followed. Archie followed behind me. We walked slowly downhill. By the time we reached the bottom of the hill it was pretty light. There in front of us stretched a swollen stream, now about fifty yards wide where it had overflowed its banks. What beautiful targets we made through that open flooded area. We spread out as much as possible so that we would not be as noticeable and vulnerable.

The water did not come through my shoes and leggings right away. Soon, however, I felt the ice cold water seeping through. Lux and Petrie, the scouts, looked around for a place to cross the main stream bed. The water had risen from the promised eighteen inches to over the height of a man. (The Germans had breached some dams upstream flooding the area.) At last they found a spot that had a barbed wire fence crossing the stream and next to it a tree with an overhanging branch. Lux and Petrie were the first to cross using the barbed wire and branch for support. We then threw their rifles to them. Lucas had the most trouble because he lost his grip on the branch. The current was so swift that it shot him against the barbed wire, where it caught him under his chin and kept him from going under. He just grabbed the barbed wire like a lifeline and pulled himself across. I benefited from the experience of the guys who preceded me. I pushed off with everything I had and was practically across before the current grabbed me. I was able to grab Petrie's hand and he pulled me out. I was lucky to get wet only up to my armpits.

The ice cold water was a real shock. When I got my rifle back, shivering and numb, I was fighting mad. I could have shot the first German I saw. After we all crossed, we started off for the village. Here and there we found German foxholes. If they had been occupied, we would have been dead ducks because they would have had perfect observation of us as we crossed the stream. Whether it was the deluge of cold rain or our artillery that made them seek shelter in the village, we could not know.

We crossed the stream much further from the village than the other units and consequently heard them firing in the village before we got there. Working our way upstream we finally came to some high ground that overlooked the village. The only way for us to get into the village was by way of a couple of hundred yards of dirt road. The trouble was that the road was very exposed to the view of any Germans in the nearby woods. We had to get into the village, so the boys took off down the road, one by one, hell bent for leather. As each man got to the middle of the road a single shot rang out.

There was a German sniper in the woods with a bolt action rifle. When my turn came I gulped and took off, I thought with everything I had. Sure enough, when I got to the middle I heard a loud crack. Then I really ran, but the road was all broken up. I tripped, fell, rolled over, was on my feet, and off again. He never did get a second shot at me. As a matter of fact, although he got a shot at each one of us, no one was hit.

The first live German soldiers I saw were lying side by side on their bellies. They were clapping their hands and feet to keep warm. They looked happy. Little Lafferty was standing guard over them with a fixed bayonet on his M-1. The Second Squad had already taken the first few houses and captured seven prisoners. A medic was attending to one of the Germans.

The First Squad, my squad, started to reinforce the Second Squad. Just before we got to where we were going we found Ortiz, a stocky Mexican, lying on his back, his uniform a red mass. He had been in a gun duel with a German in a doorway. The German shot first, hitting him in the face, knocking out some teeth. Ortiz was still game for a fight but he was hit again, this time in the arm. It was broken. He was still on his feet but not for long. The German hit him again in his side. This brought him down and put an end to the fight.

They wanted me to go back to get a medic and support. I was back in twenty minutes with the medic and support. The medic did the best he could with antiseptic powder, bandages and morphine. Sgt. Rich then asked me to stay with Ortiz until the litter bearers could pick him up.

Just before we came across Ortiz we were in the process of attacking a house. Rich told Joe to pepper the windows on the other side of the street with his B.A.R. while the other guys ran for it. Joe, his face white, put that automatic rifle through a hole in a stone wall and had that gun going like a sewing machine. Later he told me he was never more frightened in his life.

Ortiz was almost blue with the cold and the shock. About eight o'clock it stopped raining, but there was a cold November wind blowing. Like me, Ortiz had gotten a complete soaking in crossing the stream. Now he lay in his wet uniform in the cold mud. He couldn't talk very well because of the wound in his mouth. However, he made me understand that he was uncomfortable because of some K ration boxes in his pockets on which he was lying. I tried to slip the rations out of his pockets but I couldn't because his pants were wet and tight on him. The only way to get those rations out was to cut his pockets open. So that's what I did. He told me to get the coffee and chocolate out of the ration boxes and keep them. These were the most prized ingredients of our K rations.

The hours passed slowly indeed. I lay there with Ortiz expecting him to pass out anytime. About fifty yards in front of us was a board fence with some bullet holes in it. All of a sudden there was a burst of "burp" gun fire. Some branches and leaves from the tree next to us drifted down. I looked up at the board fence. It had been riddled with bullet holes. Again and again the German machine gun fired. Each time there were more holes in the fence and more leaves and twigs were clipped off the tree. I thought perhaps we could be seen by the Germans in the woods, the direction from which the machine gun fire was coming. Consequently I tried not to move, to play dead. I was concerned that the Germans might try to sneak up on us so I did turn my head from time to time.

Around noon they started throwing a terrific mortar barrage at us. There were all kinds of rubble strewn around us which gave us some protection from the flying mortar splinters. Ortiz hardly batted an eye when the mortar rounds started landing. I tried melting into the ground. Two or three landed pretty close, showering us with dirt. One time a big clod of dirt landed right on Ortiz's face. I reached over and took it off. The rest of the boys were hardly making any progress at all. One time I saw them rush across a garden firing as fast as they could. Reaching a stone wall on the other side of the garden they really put out a lot of lead. They had seen a German run into the woods and they were making it hot for him.

A member of the Second Squad came back a little later with a mattress he found. We rolled Ortiz on to the mattress to make him more comfortable. I hadn't realized how much he had bled until then. The ground under him was soaked with blood.

It was two o'clock when the litter bearers finally showed up. Ortiz had been lying there for six hours waiting for them. I told the litter bearers about the wound in his side and that they should not give him any water because of it. They loaded him on the litter and started off. They had a long way to go, all the way back to the stream where they could load him on a jeep and take him back to the Battalion Aid Station.

I ran over to the house I had seen my squad enter. Part of the Second Squad was still there. Sgt. Garvey was there lying on a pile of grain sacks with, I believe, a piece of a German rifle grenade in his groin. We covered him with grain sacks to keep him warm. The sergeant of the Third Squad had also been hit and had gone back. After a while the litter bearers came back and loaded Sgt. Garvey on a litter and took him back. I asked one of the tired-looking litter bearers how business was. He answered that they had more than they could handle.

I found out where my squad was located and went to join them there. Sgt. Rich and Corporal Phipps were standing in the doorway. I went down to the cellar where I found most of the boys. I was tired but too cold to sit down, so I walked around smoking the few cigarettes I had that had not gotten wet.

Even with all our troubles some of the boys could still joke around. "Blackie" Lincolnfelt was one boy that you could never get down. Outside mortar shells were dropping all over the place, some pretty close. Inside we tried to laugh it off. Then Willie Zinnani came down the steps with a strange look on his face. In a loud and angry voice he yelled, "Rich is dead! Rich is dead!" I couldn't believe him. I had just seen Rich a few minutes ago standing in the doorway joking with Phipps. Now I heard Phipps upstairs screaming that he could not stand the pain in his arm. Most of his right hand had been blown away. However, he had a much more serious wound in his stomach.

Rich and Phipps had been watching our own mortar shells drop where we thought the Germans had the machine gun that was holding us up. The target area wasn't more than a hundred yards away. I believe it is possible that one of our own shells might have landed short, right in front of the doorway. I believe Rich died almost immediately with holes in him from head to toe.

26

All the rest of that day I kept saying to myself, "Rich is dead! Rich is dead!" I couldn't make myself realize it was so. After they took Phipps back we all moved back a couple hundred yards and let the artillery work for a while. The new place had a great cellar. Some German troops had slept there the night before. There was straw on the floor for beds and a stove for heat and cooking. They had left in such a rush they left behind canned food and loaves of bread. The bread tasted like it was at least 50 percent sawdust.

Towards late afternoon we thought we might get to stay in that cellar for the night. The boys started to settle down. We could hardly wait for it to get dark so we could light the stove. In daylight the Germans would have shelled any house that had smoke coming from the chimney. At night, of course, they couldn't see the smoke.

We thought that we would be relieved by F Company, who was coming up. About five o'clock the cry went out, "Get them on!" That meant we were moving soon. I'd hoped we would be moving back. When we got outside I was greatly surprised to find a line of tanks with F Company riding on them, roaring into the village. Just a couple of hours before no one could show himself without causing a burst of gunfire. Now that street was a beehive of activity with tanks, jeeps and men all over the place.

We formed up on the road and moved off as it started to rain again. We went out to a hill next to the village. There we waited in the rain and gathering darkness for them to decide where we were to dig in. Some of the boys with light wounds and some others decided they needed to go back to the Battalion Aid Station.

It was after dark when they finally decided to take us out to where we were to dig in. In the darkness I lost contact with the man I was following. I stepped into one hole after another, sliding and slipping down muddy embankments. I must have wandered around for hours. I might have even been walking through the German lines and back. I certainly covered enough ground to do so.

Finally I came across a stream that seemed very much like the one we had crossed that morning. I followed it down until I saw some houses. It looked like the village we had just taken, but I was not sure.

I walked right into the village not caring whether it was in German or American hands. All I wanted was to lie down in a warm place. No one challenged me so I walked up the main street, and there silhouetted before me stood a tank. It was an American Sherman tank. What a relief!

I stumbled into a local security guard in a doorway and asked him where I could find "Easy" Company's CP. He showed me. In the doorway of the CP, which was a barn, stood Sgt. Koch, who asked me who I was. It was so dark that he felt my helmet with his hands to make sure he wasn't letting in a German.

Inside there was relief from the wind and the rain, but it was cold and damp. The floor and walls were wet. Captain Huff was half lying, half sitting in a pigsty. He picked that spot, no doubt, because the walls of the sty were made of concrete; just some added protection. Captain Huff was telling the platoon leaders the battle plan for the next day. There was to be another attack. I didn't think it was possible but my spirits sank still lower.

"Topper," our name for First Sgt. Koch, told me to hang around until I could join a group going out to my squad's position. We would be bringing them bed rolls and rations. The company radio operator had something to do so I relieved him. The radio was a SCR 300 and I knew how to operate it. After the radio operator came back I went over to a group of the boys who were preparing to heat a canteen cup of coffee. We got no water ration that night so everyone was short of water.

One of the boys contributed the coffee powder and the rest of us contributed the water we had left in our canteens. We started a waxed K ration box on fire and heated the water. Although I didn't get close enough to the burning box to get any heat, I did get satisfaction from the light of the fire. After the box had burned out we each took a shot of the hot coffee. That was the best coffee I ever tasted in my life!

About an hour or two after I got there Topper told me to grab two bed rolls and follow the carrying party out to the platoon's defensive area. It was a pretty rough trip considering I had a big, fat bed roll under each arm. The ground was slippery with mud and water. And if I let the man in front of me get more than three steps ahead of me, I would lose sight of him in the darkness. Many times I fell and did lose sight of the guy in front. Then I had to double-time in the direction we had been going and finally make contact again with the column.

When at last I did get up to our outpost I found things in a pretty bad state. The boys had started to dig holes, but at the first shovel depth they struck water so they gave it up. They were standing around shivering when I showed up with the two bed rolls.

We picked a high spot of ground near a barbed wire fence and spread the blankets right on the ground. The blankets were wet but still better than nothing. At least it broke the bitter chill of the wind. There were four of us and four blankets. Instead of two men getting together with two blankets, as was the common practice, all four of us got together between the four blankets.

We all slept on the same side, facing the same direction. Turning was impossible. I was on one end so one side of me was a lot colder than the other. My main difficulty was that there was a low spot under my head. If I let my head sink into the hole, my helmet had a tendency to flop off.

It was past one o'clock when we lay down. I think I did a lot more shivering than sleeping. It was around five o'clock and still dark when Lafferty, the platoon runner, woke us up and told us to get ready to move. A whole carton of K rations, enough for twelve men, had been brought up to us during the night. As there were now only four of us, we each took three breakfast units which we preferred, because they contained the ham and egg can and the coffee powder. We also opened the lunch and supper units for the candy and cigarettes they contained.

When the platoon got together to start our scheduled morning attack, I couldn't believe my eyes. Out of the forty men that jumped off the day before, there were now only twenty-one!

In World War II the 35th Infantry Division had a turnover of 180 percent. On average, for the entire Division, including heavy weapons, artillery and other support companies, every man who entered combat was replaced over one and a half times. For rifle companies the number was closer to four times. I was one of those replacements in a rifle company for seven of the ten months the 35th Division was in combat.

# 4 | Across Lorraine

As a result of the casualties of November 8th the platoon was reorganized. In the First Squad, my squad, both the squad leader and his assistant were now gone. As Lux seemed to have the most positive attitude he was made temporary squad leader. In the Second Squad, Mitchel replaced Garvey. In the Third Squad, Vought was replaced.

The attack jumped off as scheduled at daybreak. Our objective was a woods adjoining Malaucourt. We stopped next to a stream before entering the woods. Joe and I took the opportunity to fill our canteens from the overflowing stream.

When we got to the woods some shooting started, and we all hit the ground. It was then that one fellow noticed another who was carrying a grenade in his bandolier with the safety pin pulled out. The handle of the grenade was caught in the pocket of the bandolier, preventing it from going off. Without saying a word, the guy carefully took the grenade out and heaved it into a hole in the ground. When the grenade exploded, I thought it was a German who had thrown it at us. It wasn't until I was told what had happened that I breathed easy again. Fortunately, none of us were hurt.

We got through the woods with little opposition. Once we were fired on but we replied with such a large volume of small arms fire that they gave up. The machine gun section leader was carrying a light machine gun suspended from his shoulder by an empty ammunition belt. In this way, he could fire the machine gun from his hip. I think he may have actually hit some of the Germans. At any rate we captured seventeen of them right there.

After taking the woods, we took a town that had already been shot up by our tanks. We rounded up sixty prisoners in that town with no trouble at all. The tankers had done a good job. Instead of staying there for the night as we had hoped, we continued on and captured another town about two or three kilometers down the road. We had them on the run!

This time we were a little more fortunate in solving our housing problem. We were able to sleep indoors by sticking a machine gun on a table and pointing it out of a window of a house. There was a small stove in the house, but we couldn't get it burning very well, so we resigned ourselves to staying wet for another day. When I was awakened to do my turn over the machine gun, I got so cold I couldn't keep my teeth from chattering. I didn't stop shivering until I woke my relief and crawled under my damp blanket and generated some body heat.

The next morning we were up before dawn and attacking again. We knew the presidential election had already been held but we didn't know who had won. During the attack we came in contact with some tanks. I realized they had radios so I yelled over to one of them asking who had won the election. "Roosevelt!" he answered. I was glad. We took two towns that day.

Two afternoons later we were stopped by a German machine gun position in a woods. An artillery observation plane with three bazookas under each wing fired them at the machine gun, but didn't knock it out. We were therefore forced to dig in, in the woods.

That night we got a special treat with our rations and mail. Each squad got a bottle of French red wine through the courtesy of General Patton. After taking a swig of the wine, I tried to see by the light of the moon a letter I had received. It was my absentee ballot for the presidential election.

The following month was one of constant attacks. Every day we would take one or two villages. In the course of the day our main thought would concern the timing in taking a town. If we should take a town in the early afternoon, it could mean there was still time to gain a lot more ground even if we couldn't quite make it to the next town. This would mean we would have to sleep in foxholes that night. On the other hand, if we should capture a town just before nightfall, there would not be enough time to organize and carry through any worthwhile attack. Our worst worry was that of having to spend the night outdoors in a foxhole.

Indeed we did spend many nights in a town. Many times we were able to sleep on a dry floor and make ourselves a hot cup of coffee after coming off guard. We counted this a blessing. Sometimes someone would really hit the jackpot and find the remnants of a bed. Sleeping in a bed had two disadvantages. One is that you had to share it with as many others as could possibly fit in it with you. The other disadvantage was that the higher you were off the floor the more likely you were to collect some stray shrapnel.

Our first choice in sleeping accommodations was a good solid cellar. If we had to sleep on the ground floor, it paid to notice how many substantial walls you had between the German artillery and the place you were going to spend the night.

One night while we were in reserve we stopped in an open field. The only structure within miles was an old battered barn with half its roof and walls blown away. There wasn't enough room for all of us to get into the barn. At that point someone in command decided we had an open flank and that about half of us would need to dig in along a road. An arrangement was made whereby half the boys would stay out there for the first half of the night, and the other half of us would stay out the second half.

I was in the group to stay in the barn first. I got some blankets and tried to find a place on the cement floor to lie down. When I finally found a place to squeeze in, I discovered that the blankets were wet. With the exception of my feet, I managed to stay comparatively dry. I lay down on the cement floor with my feet wrapped in the wet blankets, covering the rest of my body with my raincoat. Pulling the raincoat over my head, I found my breath helped warm up the air under my raincoat.

I don't think I slept, because I was awake when Junior Hamilton came looking for me to go out with him to relieve our buddies. I got up shivering. I was even more miserable when I looked through a hole in the wall of the barn and saw the whole countryside was covered with a white blanket of snow. We hiked out to the foxholes and relieved the other guys.

Back in the barn, Junior Hamilton had used a sleeping bag while I had used the blankets. This time I got the sleeping bag and Junior Hamilton got the blankets. I had never used a sleeping bag, and it was too dark for me to see what I was doing. Consequently, I had a hard time getting into it. After half an hour of struggling I was comfortable. Then I began to feel deliciously warm. I was asleep in no time.

We should have taken turns staying awake, not so much because the Germans might have sneaked up on us, but because there were tanks moving around and they might have run over us in the dark. Both of us were willing to take that chance for a couple of hours of sleep. When they woke me up before dawn, I was very reluctant to leave that sack. As good as the sleeping bags were, we couldn't use them much because of the difficulty of getting out of them in a hurry.

One evening we were relieved after we had taken the town of Destry. We found ourselves a nice barn with lots of straw. They brought up hot chow for us and were doling it out at the CP in a house up the street. I was pretty hungry so I ran right over when they called us. Just as I got to the doorway of the CP with a friend at my heels there was a short shrill whistle, and then a terrific, blinding explosion. The force of the explosion propelled me through the doorway and blew the helmet off the fellow behind me. A few more shells followed the first, and then it was quiet. After we finished eating, we went back to our barn. There was a gaping big hole in the roof that hadn't been there when we went to eat.

One morning we jumped off with a railroad as our objective. We got to the railroad and captured a powerhouse. There I had the unique experience of seeing the first working electric light in Europe. After a Frenchman, who ran the place, gave us a couple of shots of cognac, we took off to clear a house a couple of hundred yards down the railroad tracks.

Lux saw a man in the house and was about to shoot when the fellow made him understand he was French. At this point Lux called me up to talk to the Frenchman. It seems there were four other men with him. They were ex–French soldiers who had been made to work for the Germans. They ran off from the Germans when we got close, and were hidden by a young French couple who lived there. I went down into the cellar where I found the four men, the French couple and two small children.

Our orders were to take all civilians to the CP, so we gave them a couple of minutes to get ready to leave. The mother was the worst problem of all. She wanted to take all kinds of junk, like fur collars and silverware. The father pushed a carriage with the older child. The mother carried the younger child in her arms. The ex–French soldiers carried their own stuff, plus some belonging to the family.

I led the procession with a rifle in one hand and a suitcase in the other. Much to our annoyance the civilians poked along slowly. We were literally on the front line and didn't relish walking around in the open. When we were a little more than halfway to the CP, the Germans put a barrage in on a hill about three hundred yards from us. When the mother saw the mountain of black smoke from the first shell, she passed me on a dead run.

We took a burning town one evening. The civilians had all herded themselves together in the church. I had gone for rations to the CP and found it was no longer there. The barn next to where the CP had been was burning. The CP had been moved elsewhere. In the barn were animals making all kinds of sounds. Outside stood a G.I. watching. He turned to me and said, "Too bad they let the barn burn so far without letting the animals out or shooting them."

In the now smoldering former CP, a woman was trying to get into the cellar. In answer to my questions, she told me she wanted to get some possessions down there. I told her it was too dangerous; that the house would be completely engulfed in a few minutes. She took my advice and went away crying. Half the houses in the town were completely ruined by shells or fire.

Once we were halfway through taking a village when a Frenchman ran out of a house with a bottle of cognac. In no time there was a crowd around him. All of a sudden, there was a streak of white tracers dividing the street. A German had opened up with a machine gun. Before the echo of the first burst had died away, there was no one on the street. I ducked into a nearby house and waited. After a while it was decided we would use that house as a platoon CP for the night.

Fitzgerald, who had just come back from the hospital, was then the Platoon Guide. Wanting to demonstrate his efficiency, he inquired whether the cellar had been searched yet. No one answered so he asked one of the boys for a grenade and proceeded to throw it down into the basement. The grenade having gone off and feeling more secure he prepared to spend the night in the house. In a couple of minutes we noticed smoke coming from the cellar. There had been straw down there and the grenade had set it afire. We had to find ourselves another home for the night.

Thanksgiving Day we attacked over a flooded lowland. The Germans had blown a dam somewhere, turning pastures into lakes three and four feet deep. We tried to walk on the high spots but once in a while we would go in waste deep.

One time we came to a stream that paralleled our line of advance. Fitzgerald alone jumped across it right away. He advanced up the left bank while the rest of us continued up the right bank. After a while we came to some brush, at which point Fitzgerald wanted some of us to cross to the other side of the stream. Now, however, the stream was much wider and probably six or seven feet deep. He caught my eye first so he ordered me to come across. I argued with him and stalled for time any way I could. He had a big branch he wanted me to grab. He was going to pull me across. There was a strong current and I was encumbered by all kinds of equipment. Chances are that I might have drowned had I done what he asked.

Finally I couldn't put him off any longer so I started very slowly. I had just about one foot knee deep in water when someone up front found a bridge across the stream. Boy, what a relief! Some time later, Fitzgerald was made a P.F.C. and was transferred to the wire section where he could do no harm.

Thanksgiving Day evening we were relieved and allowed to go back to where we started the attack. My clothes being wet, my legs became chafed. Fortunately there was a barn close by that was all but burned to the ground. It had one stone wall still standing and a smoldering hay stack nearby. I got between the hay stack and the wall. In about half an hour, with steam coming off me, I was almost dry. The next day I went to the Aid Station and got some salve for my legs which did the trick.

**It must have been around Thanksgiving time when we got these cards to send home. I was happy for the opportunity to strike a cheerful note in the mail I was sending home.**

The day after Thanksgiving we got our Thanksgiving dinner. I found a big plate that I used instead of the conventional G.I. mess gear. They heaped the plate so high with turkey and other things that it literally overflowed. I ate so much that I could hardly move.

Attacking at that time became somewhat easier than in the first days of November. The Germans had decided to retreat and were only fighting rear guard actions. In one attack on a town we were lucky enough to be in reserve. In that capacity we followed up the two attacking platoons. We thought we would have no trouble at all when we saw the attacking platoons enter the town with hardly any shooting.

Our platoon started to follow the others into the town when the Germans put a terrific artillery barrage down on us while we were in the open. The only visible protection was a cemetery wall so I ran for it. While running, I heard a shell coming right at me. Then I saw it explode on a building about two hundred yards to my left. The next instant I was on the ground with shrapnel screaming over my head. I had hit the ground between the time I saw the shell hit and the time it took for the shrapnel to reach me.

I got up and ran for the cemetery wall. On the way, I saw a foxhole that some

German had dug and slept in the night before. I dived into it, catching my breath and thanking God that no one had shot the German who dug this hole.

In the previous town, I had picked up a German blanket and put it into a school bag that I found. I hooked the school bag over the bayonet on my belt. In that way I could get rid of it in a hurry in case I ever wanted to. At this point mobility was paramount so I discarded the blanket. I had picked up the blanket because getting our bed rolls at night had proved to be an uncertain thing. Usually they came late at night and often they were wet. Moreover, we never got as many blankets as we wanted. Many times we supplemented our blankets with the bed clothes of neighboring houses.

One night after I had dug my hole and settled down for the night, Watson got me up and told me to go on an outpost with Luke, Joe and another guy. Luke was to be in charge so Watson told him where to go and what to do. We were supposed to go to a crossroad and make contact with a neighboring battalion. A patrol from that battalion would come to us every two hours.

We went out there and dug a narrow three-man hole because we would always need one man on guard. At ten o'clock a patrol was supposed to contact us. They didn't. At eleven o'clock Watson and Henley came up to see how we were doing. When Watson saw we had gone to the wrong place, he decided to personally go out to the proper contact point in time for the next contact.

Watson was nursing a bottle in his field jacket. Luke had a bottle sticking out of each of his two jacket pockets. Luke, Watson and Henley went off quietly to make the twelve o'clock contact. When I went on guard at one o'clock they were still not back. I began to think they might have been captured. Just before I was ready to wake my relief I heard some voices in the distance. Soon the voices were much closer. I was puzzled because no one would talk out loud on the front line at night. I was ready for anything.

Now I see three silhouettes stagger over the skyline. Luke was waving his P-38 pistol and shouting defiance to everybody. Watson, too, was talking pretty loudly. Henley was supporting both of them. Watson greets me with, "Have a drink!" Henley tells me that they had gone to the appointed spot and found some straw in which to lie and wait. It got cold so they took a shot to keep warm. Then they began drinking without an excuse. Henley had abstained for some reason.

I was really surprised at Watson. He was an unusually competent guy. He had been running the platoon ever since Lt. Tompkins developed his heavy cold during our first attack. Luke, I knew, got drunk at every opportunity. The first thing Luke did was to urinate while we were standing around talking. Watson tried to follow suit but he couldn't manage to unbutton his pants so he got himself all wet. Henley took Watson back to the CP and we put Luke in our hole. Luke was no good to us anymore as far as taking his turn at guard.

To top everything off Luke got sick while Joe and I were in the hole with him. Joe managed to get Luke's helmet under his face just as Luke threw up. What a stink! We were wedged in there so tightly we could hardly turn. There was no escaping the odor. We were supposed to stay there until seven o'clock, but since we were not accomplishing anything we went back about five.

A few days later we got what I had been dreaming about. That was Corps reserve. That meant the entire division would be off the front line. We spent a couple of days practicing crossing rivers in assault boats, firing the bazooka at a knocked-out tank, and worst of all, how to take a pill box. We practiced on actual Maginot Line fortifications. We blew them sky high. This, of course, gave us the impression that we would be used as a spearhead in cracking the Siegfried Line in Germany. We were formed into combat teams of about ten men with the following equipment: bazookas, shaped explosive charges, and flame throwers. I drew a flame thrower.

When we were not training, we could go to a movie in a barn or go through the Red Cross Clubmobile. Here you would get two doughnuts and half a canteen cup of coffee. The Red Cross girls played popular records on a public address system, which was as much appreciated as the doughnuts and coffee. I went through the line several times until I got my fill of music and food. The rest of the time we spent cooking our own little delicacies, including fried chicken and French-fried potatoes.

After a week of training we started moving again. For a while we thought we would be following an attacking regiment. In fact we did this for two days. Then one night they asked us for an ammunition report, and we knew we would not be in reserve much longer. Joe got a lucky break that same night: a three day pass to Nancy. Half an hour after the ammunition report went in, the company runner came over to tell us to pick up the ammunition. Instead of the usual two bandoliers we were to carry three.

Our objective was to be the city of Sarreguemines which was over the Saar River. The only way we had of crossing the river was over the remnants of a blown up bridge. Besides our regular rations we got one day's emergency concentrated chocolate D ration. After we crossed the river we were to drop one of the three bandoliers in a reserve ammunition pool. We didn't know whether our supply line over the bridge might be cut. Therefore we had to be prepared to hold out for a couple of days on the other side of the river.

At two o'clock the next morning we started out with our overload of reserve food, ammunition, overcoats and overshoes. We had an eight mile hike before we hit the bridge. A couple of hours into the hike we passed through a battery of artillery in the process of sending out the mail. We could hear someone in the plotting tent calling out firing data. Minutes later three guns let go at one time with a terrific flash and roar.

In another hour we reached the bridge. It was a mass of twisted steel, but there was a makeshift foot bridge of boards over the parts that couldn't be negotiated by an overloaded infantryman. The first thing I saw when we finally got across was a dead German. We had gotten the impression that this was Germany on this side of the river. I felt a certain gratification. Now no more French people would suffer the ravages of war.

We were led into a small forest at the edge of the river where we waited for dawn. As soon as it got light enough we started across an open pasture. Every minute it got lighter. We got about one third of the way across when a 20 MM automatic canon started firing at us. He was shooting high and off to our right. We didn't waste time getting into the first houses of the city. Off on our left there was a big pottery factory that was giving F Company serious trouble.

Watson was pretty aggressive that morning so we kept going through houses one after the other without encountering any resistance. Then I see Lux in the doorway of the next building in front of us. All of a sudden there is a burst of gunfire and I see chips flying off the wall over Lux's head. Later Lux told me he had seen two Germans and asked them to surrender. One of the Germans threw his hands up. The other German let go a burst from his "burp" gun. Lux returned the fire winging one of them. At this point, Watson had us hold up. He then sent a man back to see where the rest of the company was located. When he came back we found out we were the only platoon this far into the city. We didn't have support on either side of us. If the Germans knew the true situation they could have easily surrounded and captured us.

Right about now I found out that Sarreguemines is a French city and not a German city. Many inhabitants, without realizing the danger, poked their heads out of windows. One bearded Frenchman opened the shutters of an upper story window, stood what must have been his grandchild on the window sill and, pointing to me, exclaimed to the child, "Les Americains! Les Americains!" It was a wonder more civilians weren't hurt. At a distance we couldn't tell whether it was a German soldier or a civilian watching us.

The Second Squad had a lucky break. They stopped in a cellar across the street where some civilians cooked them a meal of ham and eggs and supplemented it with a bottle of cognac. At the same time my squad cooked our K rations in the house we occupied.

After a couple of hours the rest of the battalion came up on a line with us and we continued to clear our strip of buildings. Most of the civilians took refuge in air raid shelters and basements. On leaving their homes they locked the doors to avoid being robbed. However, when we came to a locked door we had to break it down to see if there wasn't a German hiding inside. I, personally, must have knocked down about twenty doors that day. I made the discovery that not all doors are as substantial as they seem. Most of the doors I hit went down after about three good whacks of my shoulder.

In the afternoon we came across a civilian who said he had two German soldiers in his basement who wanted to surrender. We approached the place carefully. Outside were strewn guns and equipment. We yelled for them to come out. They answered, but they didn't come out. After a lot of talk in which neither side understood the other, they finally came out with their hands in the air and their faces white as chalk. They didn't know whether we would shoot them or not. One of them was an SS man. I was surprised to see his slight physique, which was unusual for the SS.

We were about halfway through the city when it got dark. They led us back to a large apartment house where we were to spend the night. There were no beds in the room we were in, so I went up one flight and found myself a feather tick to sleep on. A little while later a girl came in and asked what we were going to do with the feather tick. I told her we would put it back when we left. This satisfied her. Meantime I engaged her in conversation and found out she was my age, twenty-two, had three years of medical school in Strasbourg and wasn't bad-looking. In five minutes we were great friends but I was so tired I broke off the conversation and went to sleep.

The next morning we started to clear the rest of the city. We didn't have as much to be concerned about anymore, because the engineers had built a bridge over the river and the tanks had rolled into town. We no longer had to fear being cut off by German armor. Around noontime we held up for a while. We hadn't gotten any water in the past day so when I found a water pump there was a big rush by our guys to get water. The Frenchman who owned the well was so enthusiastic about our using it, he nearly broke his back pumping it for us.

I told one of the boys where to find me and went into one of the houses. There was hot water on the stove so I asked the girl there for some of it. She not only gave me the water but also gave me a cup and spoon. I dissolved half a lemonade powder packet in the water and sipped it. The girl told me they had buried a child in the garden ten days before. Owing to the fighting they couldn't get the body to the cemetery, so the garden served as a temporary expedient. I was halfway through the cup of hot lemonade when I heard someone outside yell, "Get 'em on!" I left the lemonade with the girl and went outside just in time to get into the formation as it went by.

Our next stop was a few blocks down the street near an old French barracks.

We went into a house and took over a couple of rooms with the idea of spending the night there. We even negotiated a big pot of rabbit and potato stew. As soon as we got settled, I went outside and looked around. Down the street there was a French girl giving away cake to G.I.s. I went over and got myself a piece.

While I was eating the cake, a woman came over to tell me she had a wounded German soldier in her house and that he needed aid. I went back to our Aid Station, got an Aid Man and brought him to the woman's house. All the Aid Man could do was to give the German soldier a shot of morphine. He told me the German had been shot in the stomach and would not last through the night. When I got back to our house I found all the boys outside with their equipment on, ready to move. We were not going to spend the night there after all. Instead we were to move to the outskirts of the city.

I had picked up a German helmet with an SS symbol on it. I hung it on my belt so I could throw it away if the going got tough. If possible, I was intending to send it home later. Every Frenchman who recognized the SS insignia got a big kick out of seeing it dangling from my belt.

Again we got the signal to hold up. I walked over to the closest building in order to lean my pack against it. An old man and a girl were watching us from a window in the building. I lifted the helmet so that they could see the SS insignia on it. When the girl saw it she burst out laughing. That broke the ice and we started talking.

After a couple of minutes there came the whine of some incoming mail. I immediately made for the cellar of the house. There on the steps going down, I met the same girl. While the barrage came in we were able to talk and become friends. Her name was Raymonde. We talked for a long time, and I began to feel sorry that we would soon have to move again.

At this point Lux came in and told me to ask Raymonde if she could put six of us up for the night. When I asked her she replied there was room for only four men. We went into the bedroom where we saw two double beds covered with loose plaster. A shell had landed right outside the window spraying everything with shrapnel. Raymonde insisted on cleaning the plaster from the beds. We told her we would do it but she replied that cleaning was a woman's job and not a man's. We went right to sleep because we had to get up again at around four o'clock.

At four o'clock our platoon relieved the Second Platoon who had dug foxholes in a field about half a mile down the road. The man I relieved had dug a shallow, muddy hole. As there was no artillery coming in, I decided to sit on the edge of the hole instead of lying in it. I had an extra English rain cape that I put over my head so that I could keep the warmth of my breath. One of the other boys was on guard, so I dozed off. After a long time it started to change from the darkness of night to the grey of dawn. When I thought I could get away with it, I lit a cigarette underneath the rain cape. A cigarette when you are cold, wet and miserable is worth a great deal.

When it got light, I began to improve the hole I was in. I tried to clean the mud from the bottom of the hole but it was only a temporary measure, because the surface water kept coming in. Looking around, I saw a section of fence lying close by. I jumped out and dragged it up to the hole. Widening and deepening the hole in the right places, I was able to fit the fence into the bottom of the hole. This gave me a duck board floor. Now I could stretch out in the protection of the hole without wallowing in the cold mud. Around noon we were relieved by the Third Platoon. We returned to Sarreguemines where we could take it easy until we were scheduled to return to the line.

When I met Raymonde again, I happened to scratch my whiskers, which were itching me. This prompted her to ask me if I wanted some hot water to shave. I told her to bring it on. In twenty minutes, I was clean shaven and eating breakfast at the family table. Raymonde was living in the cellar of the house with her mother and father. They had two big double beds down there, plus a stove and table and chairs. All except one window were barricaded with heavy logs. The other window had a removable barricade that was taken away during daylight hours. In short, they had a giant deluxe foxhole.

Of course, the family didn't have too much to eat themselves so I brought rations with me whenever they invited me to eat with them. Their main staples were pea soup and bread, which tasted very good to me. No doubt K rations were a deluxe item with them, considering the can of meat, cigarettes and candy they contained. The old man still had some good cognac that he offered me whenever no one else was around. He wanted to make it last as long as possible. They were all very friendly and tried to cheer me up anyway they could.

That night we went on the line again. This time we took over another sector where there were no holes. It was raining, black as pitch, and thoroughly miserable when we started digging. We couldn't see how to dig so it had to be done by feel. Every time I stuck my shovel into the ground I had to feel if it was in the right place. Half the time, there was no dirt on the shovel when I thought I was throwing dirt out of the hole. We finally settled for a hole that was very narrow and only six inches deep. We dug the hole as much to keep out of the biting wind as for protection from shrapnel.

Again, we returned to Sarreguemines, this time to a house across the street from Raymonde's. After a couple of hours of sleep I went across the street to kill some time with Raymonde. She told me she had four brothers, all of whom were in the French army. One of her brothers was killed by an American air raid on this city. My French was getting better all the time so we had little trouble understanding each other.

One night the boys dug up a couple of bottles of red wine, which they were emptying. When I came in there was just one bottle left. They handed it to me, asking me to taste it to see if it was okay. I smelled it, took a sip and then a good healthy shot. It was okay. I passed the bottle around but they all had enough, so I took it with me when I went on guard. The guard post was upstairs at a window. There was a desk that I pushed in front of the window. I sat down in a chair I had put in front of the desk and then put my feet up on the desk. I had the use of a Browning Automatic Rifle which I put across my lap. Finally, I took a good long swig of wine and considered I was open for business. It certainly was tough to keep from falling asleep.

The next day we moved back to Sarreguemines. That afternoon, they asked for an ammunition report. When I headed over to Raymonde's, Heady and Luke tagged along, mainly with the idea of getting a shot of cognac. We sat around, talked and showed snap shots. Heady, who seemed like he was only a few years over thirty, amazed everyone with pictures of his family, which included five children.

That was the last time I had dinner in France for a while.

# 5 | INTO GERMANY

We left Sarreguemines in the evening and hiked about three kilometers south along the Blies River to Frauenberg. Here I spent about five hours in a bed in a house. We got up about four o'clock, cooked a quick K ration breakfast, and started moving. They led us down to a bridge across the Blies River. We moved at a snail's pace as we approached the bridge, because of the large volume of traffic crossing the bridge with us. When I actually got on the bridge, I ran at top speed, nearly beating the Sherman tank that roared across with me. A bridge is no place to be when the enemy knows that it is the only artery to a bridgehead across the river. When I stepped off that bridge, I stepped on to the sacred soil of the "Faterland!"

Once on the other side of the river, we moved uphill where some other outfit had dug in. By this time, it was getting light very fast. Most of the boys sought out ditches, holes, folds in the ground or anything that would give them a little defilade, where they could stretch out for a couple of minutes rest.

I remember Archie Campbell and Willie Zinnani taking their new overshoes off and throwing them away. They had looked at the open hill that we were sched-uled to take and decided they didn't want the extra weight on their feet. I was tempted to do the same thing. Later I was alternately sorry and glad that I didn't.

The "big picture" for the plan of the attack was to send some other outfit directly against the front of the small town in the valley while our battalion was to get around the back of the town by going over the hill that overlooked it. The plan looked good on paper. The trouble was that the Germans had thought of the same possibility and had zeroed in every mortar and artillery piece they had on that hill in anticipation of just such an attack.

Too soon it was light enough to get started. Walking slowly up the hill, it began to look as if it might not be so bad after all. We had gotten no small arms fire from the group of houses on top of the hill. Our medium and heavy artillery had blasted that hilltop so heavily that it seemed that the Germans could not hold it.

About halfway up the hill the first mortar shell dropped in on us. Mortar shells travel comparatively slowly without making the shrill whine of the faster artillery shell. This quiet approach does not give the warning that artillery shells give. This warning whine usually gives you enough time to hit the ground before the explosion. While mortar shells approach more quietly they were usually launched several at a time, so we all hit the dirt immediately after the first one exploded.

The first shell was followed by a second, a third, and then it seemed as if it was raining mortar shells. We were caught on a perfectly smooth grassy slope. There wasn't any kind of defilade within two hundred yards. To get up and run would have been certain suicide. The sound of shrapnel going over my head was continuous.

There was nothing to do but lie there and hope that the next one wouldn't come any closer than the last. I pushed my face down into the ground and tried to pull my helmet down around my ears. A couple of shells must have landed within twenty feet of me. I was showered with clods of earth. For even more protection, I held the receiver of my rifle in front of my head.

How long that mortar barrage lasted, I can't really tell; probably not much more than a quarter of an hour. It seemed much, much longer. After a while the shells were coming in more sporadically, so Watson decided we should move on. He signaled us to get up and continue up the hill. I passed one fellow who didn't get up. As we got close to the top of the hill we began to find huge shell holes that were probably made by our own 240 MM howitzers. They were a particularly welcome sight. I could run from one to another.

While in one of these huge shell holes, the shelling increased in intensity. I curled up in the bottom of the hole, trying not to get too wet from the pool of water right in the center. Then, a shell landed right at the edge of the hole, and I felt a burning sensation in my leg. I had never been hit before. This began to look as if it might result in a hospital stay; that is, if I could get out of this situation alive. I didn't want to look around at my leg for fear of what I might see, so I felt my leg with my hand. There was no blood. I brought myself to look at my leg. There was only a tiny hole in my pants. However it still burned. Then it was time to move again, so I got up and took off.

We were getting closer to the buildings at the top of the hill. Again, the mortar shells started dropping. I dived into a smaller shell hole, probably made by a 105 MM shell. It was just large enough to get most of my body in. The ground at the bottom of the hole was split into clods of mud. With my fingers I tore at the clods directly under my face. I put the clods all around my head, leaving my head almost completely surrounded by earth. Then I began seeing to the rest of my body, wriggling around to get as low as possible.

Now we were getting only sporadic shells, one every minute or two. I began enlarging my hole with my shovel. I had to lie on my side, which made me a little more vulnerable. I now discovered that I could actually hear the mortar rounds being fired off in the distance. I counted eighteen seconds from the time the mortar shell was launched until it landed. That meant I could safely work on expanding my hole for twelve seconds and still have at least five seconds to get down in the hole before the shell hit.

By the time the hole was deep enough to give me decent protection, the decision was made to take the buildings at the top of the hill. Putting my shovel back into its carrier, I noticed that the front sight on my rifle had been knocked way off center. Before I could do anything about it we were running for the buildings. When I got right up to them I saw there was very little left of what once was a very comfortable farming community. There wasn't a single whole roof left out of the dozen or more buildings.

After running up to one house I dived into a large shell crater next to it. From there, I rolled through a hole in the foundation right into the basement. After I caught my breath, I banged the front sight of my rifle back to its approximate previous position with a big rock. The accuracy of the sight was now a big open question. The cellar soon filled with guys coming in the same way I did. I pulled the pants leg out of my boot and looked at my leg. I was disappointed. There was only a red welt there.

Doc (that's what we called him) soon came in through the same hole. His face was somewhere between green and white. He told us about a guy he had just treated. It was one of our machine gunners. A shell had landed between his legs, tearing most of one away. Doc had tried to stop the bleeding, but couldn't. There were just too many holes in him. In five minutes he was dead; the machine gun was still in his hands.

After a long while, we reorganized. Our platoon was given a building facing the direction from which the mortar fire was coming. We assembled in the cellar and sat down to rest. Personally, I didn't think we should stay there. The German mortar and artillery observers had perfect observation on us. They could see our slightest move.

When it started to get dark, Watson came in with the glad tidings that we would outpost the hill that night. The first thing I did was to claim a solid corner of the cellar as my personal CP by laying my pack there. Next, I crawled upstairs where I found a section of a mattress. I put the mattress section on the coal pile in the corner of the cellar that I had chosen. I tried it out for size. It was too short. Curling up, my head still hung over one end of the mattress and my feet hung over the other end. My pack, placed on the coal, became my pillow and the problem was solved.

We had to make more room in the place so we could all lie down. It seemed that there were hundreds of bottles of all shapes lying around. A couple of us started shoving the bottles through the cellar's windows. We soon had all the windows blocked with bottles. When it got dark we went outside and piled dirt on the bottles to make the windows light proof. The stairway upstairs was blocked by the collapsed roof. The only possible entrance was through the hole in the basement wall.

After dark, four of us were taken out to the slope of the hill and told to dig in. We had to be out there to prevent infiltration by the Germans. I suggested we look for a shell hole to give us a start. I stumbled into a big 240 MM shell hole. There was enough room for all of us to sit down in it, but no more. For about an hour we tried enlarging the shell hole with our shovels. At that point we decided it wasn't safe to make noise anymore so we sat down and waited for twelve o'clock, when we would be relieved. At midnight we were relieved by some fellows from another platoon. We didn't waste time starting back to the cellar. It was extremely cold and I was sleepy, so I lay down right away. Some of the others made themselves hot coffee before turning in.

I wasn't sleeping very well when, around two o'clock, I heard gunfire break out not far away. I could distinguish one of our B.A.R.s and a German "burp" gun. In a little while I could hear the sound of footsteps right outside our house. Whether the person out there wore olive drab or "feldgrau" I didn't know, and I wasn't going to find out.

Even in daylight the entrance to our cellar was hard to find. On this black night it would have been impossible. If we kept quiet and there were Germans out there, they would pass us by. If we went out to see who it was we would have to make noise, and they would get in the first shots. It was also probable that a G. I. might shoot at a noise made in a place he had previously thought to be unoccupied.

When I heard the bottles outside the window being moved, I started thinking of what I would do if a grenade came through the window. I planned to flatten out against the wall and put the mattress on my other side. The mattress might slow up a piece of shrapnel enough to help. No matter how little protection I could get, I would take advantage of it. The noise and shooting soon stopped and I dozed off again in about a half hour.

It was late morning when I finally got up and started to make my breakfast. It wasn't possible to bring up all the water we needed, so we were limited to a single canteen cup of water for the entire day. As for bringing up the bed rolls, with the exposed position we were in, that was really impossible. That meant we had to try sleeping in this cold December weather without blankets.

I decided that I would eat only two meals a day because there was only enough water for two cups of coffee. For the first meal I ate the breakfast unit of the K ration plus half the cheese of the lunch unit. The cheese I cut into slabs and put between two dog biscuits that came with the ration. I ate this with the heated tin of ham and eggs. There was a packet of soluble coffee in the breakfast unit that made an excellent half cup of hot coffee. For dessert, there was a bar of pressed fruit. For the second meal, I had the other half of the cheese with the supper unit's tin of corned pork loaf. Under most conditions, I would have thrown the corned pork loaf away. Now, however, I had half an onion that one of the boys had tossed to me. The supper unit didn't have coffee but I had foreseen situations like this one and had a reserve of about eight packets of soluble coffee in my shirt pocket. Outside of a little thirst, my stomach was well taken care of. After each meal I had a cigarette. The candy ration helped during the long nights. Each of us stood an hour's guard during the day at the hole in the cellar wall. During my turn at guard some of our units on our right flank launched an attack. First the P-47s came over and strafed the edge of the woods about a mile away. The red tracers were plainly visible, and the sound of their machine guns was frightening. Next came a formation of Sherman tanks crawling forward, firing their canons and machine guns. Our artillery that had been ripping the place apart now stopped, for now it was the infantry's turn.

In France we had attacked woods like this with no support and had taken them, but this was different. This was the first time these Germans were fighting for the very soil of the "Faterland!" There had been sufficient time for them to get ready for us, and they were very well dug in. The infantry barely got started. They just couldn't make any headway.

That night they moved the Second Platoon to another sector so now they wouldn't relieve us at midnight. Instead we were going to be out there for all of the fourteen hour night. This time I went out there a little better prepared. I managed to find a thin wedge-shaped section of a mattress that I intended using as a pillow. I took it out there with me together with an English-type rain cape that I had found.

When we got out there, I dug a ledge in the side of the shell crater. I put the pillow on the ledge and fastened the rain cape at the edge of the crater so that it covered the ledge. When I was finished with my turn at guard, I squeezed in between the rain cape and the pillow and tried to sleep. If I didn't always succeed in sleeping, at least I did feel a little bit warmer.

There were four of us in the hole; Luke, Joe, one other guy, and myself. Luke was the only one with a watch, but it didn't have a luminous dial, so we had no means of telling when to wake up our relief. We just had to guess when our hour was up so we could wake the next guy. Every fifteen minutes or so a machine gun battery on the other side of the river, in France, sent a stream of tracers into the town in the valley. Once we thought it must be time to go back to the house, so Luke looked at his watch by the light of a match under his raincoat. It was only a little past four o'clock. We couldn't leave until seven.

After returning to the house we made and ate breakfast, and then went to sleep. Getting up about midday, I thought it would be a good idea if we could have an indoor toilet. As it stood, it was not possible to go outside without being in plain sight of the Germans on the next hill. In a pile of junk in the next room I found a big pot marked "Kartoffeln," or potatoes. Upstairs I found the lid of a rubbish can. The potato pot was big enough to last a week for our purposes. Putting the pot and lid in the adjoining junk room gave us a very practical indoor toilet.

When it came time for my hour of daytime guard, I went up to the guard post, which was the hole in the wall of the basement. There I found a copy of *Stars & Stripes* that had been brought up during the night. There was a big map on the front page. It showed where von Rundstedt was making a big hole in our line up north. This did not look so good. This seemed to be the hardest fighting we had yet had.

That night we went out again. This time we were a little more alert because one of the men at the outpost had been captured the night before without a shot being fired. The night passed slower than ever but finally it was time to go back. We put our stuff on and headed back to our house. We were almost at the house when one of the F Company guards in the building to the left of ours called out, "Halt!" We waited for him to give the "sign" so we could give him the "counter sign." Instead we heard some muttering and then a pop, followed by a hissing sound. We all knew what that meant. He had tossed a grenade at us and it was going to go off in about four seconds.

Naturally we all hit the ground and sure enough, the grenade went off, sending fragments whining over our heads. We were lucky. The fellow who threw the grenade, a green replacement, was wearing an overcoat. This handicapped him in throwing the grenade. It fell far short of its intended mark which was us. There

48

had also been a lot of masonry rubble on the ground, which probably stopped most of the low flying fragments. After the grenade went off Luke got up and cursed the thrower in a very loud voice.

Later, after I got up from my morning snooze, I heard the good news. We were going to be relieved that night. That night we took all our equipment with us when we went out to our holes. In about an hour a platoon of riflemen from the 44th Division came up and told us they were taking over. We gave the hole over to them with pleasure. We took off down the hill following the same route we had taken when we attacked it some days before. We got to Haberkirchen, the town on the German side of the river and then crossed back over the Blies River into the town of Frauenberg in France. We went back to the same house we had stayed in for the few hours before the attack.

As soon as we got to the house, I relieved the guard at the door who was acting as local security so that he could eat his supper. In half an hour I, too, was relieved so that I could make and eat my own supper. I had hardly finished eating when they told us to "Get 'em on!" and get out on the road. We started back to Sarreguemines. Halfway back there was a sudden crash of machine gun fire and the road was lit up with several streams of red tracers passing over our heads. Naturally, without thinking, the column melted into the ditches on both sides of the road. Then we realized that these were our own machine guns and this was the same battery that had been delivering harassing fire on that little German town in the valley.

Once in Sarreguemines we got on trucks and started moving back into the interior of France.

# 6 | THE BATTLE OF THE BULGE

The trucks rolled north all night. It was an extremely cold night. All the fields were covered with frost. Toward the last hours of darkness we heard aircraft overhead. Anti-aircraft guns opened up and we stopped. The sky was filled with tracers all crossing at one point. Most of the boys hardly paid any attention, being asleep with blankets over their heads. I folded my blanket in half and wrapped it like a shawl around my head. I wanted to be prepared if any of those German planes were going to make a pass at our convoy.

The driver, a black man, got out of the cab of the truck and prepared to add his bit with the .50 caliber machine gun mounted on top of the cab. He kept repeating to himself, "Just let me see one of those bloody buggers!"

When the firing stopped we started again, rolling into Metz just before dawn. We pulled into a large drill field completely surrounded by stone barracks several stories high. We got off the trucks and were led into one of the buildings where we prepared to bed down for the night. I decided to explore the area to see if I could find something to sleep on. Sure enough, I found a little straw mattress which made things a lot pleasanter.

They woke us up at ten o'clock the next morning for a breakfast of hot cakes that really hit the spot after over a week of K rations. That day Watson was made platoon leader of the weapons platoon and we got Whitman to replace him. Whitman had just come back from the hospital. One of the new replacements became the B.A.R. man and Joe became a rifleman. The second in command of the First Squad was also replaced.

On the following day they put a bunch of us on all kinds of details designed to make the place more livable. This didn't bother us because we thought these were sure signs that we would stay here for a while. I was stuck on a coal shoveling detail. Four of us got on a truck and were driven to a railroad yard where we pulled up alongside a railroad car full of coal. In less than an hour we filled the truck full of coal and started back.

On the way back we talked the driver into stopping at a little tavern for a couple of glasses of beer, a real treat. We also picked up a couple of loaves of French bread at only ten francs (twenty cents) apiece. The bread proved to be especially welcome when I found a package from home waiting for me. It had a jar of jam in it. The jar was wrapped in the front page of the *New York Post* with the headline, "METZ FALLS!"

The next day was Christmas Day. There were to be only two meals. For breakfast we had ham and eggs made to order, bread and jam and coffee. It was the best breakfast I had in Europe! Aside from the good meals, I also received packages from home to round out my diet. In the afternoon came the climax to the day's gastronomic orgy, Christmas dinner. The menu consisted of a big slab of turkey plus a drumstick, potatoes, cranberry sauce, gravy, greens, fruit cocktail, peaches, bread and jam, and a choice of coffee or lemonade.

The portions were as large as you wanted. All you had to do was ask. I refused a pass to Metz so that I wouldn't miss this chow.

After smoking a cigar, I put on my overcoat and along with some friends strolled across the parade ground to a large auditorium. It had been built by or for an SS regiment that had used it not long before. There we saw a pretty good movie. After the movie we strolled back in the moonlight, much as we had done during basic training in the States.

We went to bed rather early because of the poor lighting facilities. Around midnight I was awakened by a lot of confused noises coming from some replacements that had just arrived. Instead of letting them bed down immediately, Whitman, our new Platoon Sergeant, was making the replacements separate their belongings into stuff that they would carry into combat and the stuff they would leave behind in their barracks bags. I couldn't see the sense in making them do it in the middle of the night. It could certainly wait for morning.

At four o'clock in the morning they woke us up amid the rumble of trucks on the parade ground. We ate hot chow after which we handed in our mess gear, a

## HEADQUARTERS
## THIRD UNITED STATES ARMY

T O each officer and soldier in the Third United States Army, I wish Merry Christmas. I have full confidence in your courage, devotion to duty, and skill in battle. We march in our might to complete victory. May God's blessing rest upon each of you on this Christmas Day.

G. S. PATTON, JR.,
Lieutenant General,
Commanding, Third United States Army

## PRAYER

A LMIGHTY and most merciful Father, we humbly beseech Thee, of Thy great goodness, to restrain these immoderate rains with which we have had to contend. Grant us fair weather for Battle. Graciously hearken to us as soldiers who call upon Thee that armed with Thy power, we may advance from victory to victory, and crush the oppression and wickedness of our enemies, and establish Thy justice among men and nations. Amen.

During the Battle of the Bulge, General George Patton wished his Third Army a Merry Christmas; on the other side, a prayer. General Patton had these greetings (2¼" × 3¾") distributed to us in December 1944. I pasted mine in a photo album with transparent tape around the borders. After 50 years the tape grew very dark, so I cut it off and enlarged the rest about 60 percent. The prayer was an appeal to providence for better weather.

52

sure sign we were going into combat. We made up our bed rolls, drew bandoliers, grenades and rations and sat down to wait. In a few minutes it came: "Get 'em on!" We loaded on the trucks and were out of Metz before daybreak.

We rode all day. Soon we knew from the signs on the stores in the towns that we were in Belgium. Late in the afternoon we finally detrucked in a small village covered with snow. From the people in the village we learned that we were now in Luxemburg in the Ardennes. A quartering party found us a place to stay with some civilians. We were issued gas masks, which were not in use up to that time. This was for purposes of identification. Some Germans were wearing American uniforms so the possession of a gas mask would show who was a G.I. and who was a German.

You didn't need to be a genius to know that things would be popping soon, so we bedded down early. Around eight o'clock came the request for an ammunition report. Whitman went down to the CP for orders and came back with the news that we would be jumping off in the morning. He also told us we might have to wade through a stream eighteen inches deep.

Around four o'clock in the morning we got up, made our bed rolls and carried them down to the CP. We then got on trucks and went down the road about four miles. Here we got off the trucks and started to walk. When daybreak came we were up to a river but the bridge across it was still intact so there was no wading that day.

I went across the bridge in a big hurry because it was out in the open and could be seen from points miles away. On the other side we began climbing a winding road up a high hillside. Following me was one of the new men, Emerson. He was a good-looking guy and he seemed somewhat bewildered. The dead German along the road didn't make him feel any better. In one place in some bushes, I saw and heard a wounded and unconscious German. He was wearing parts of an American uniform so our medics couldn't find time to take care of him.

Every once in a while we would stop, at which time I would sit in the lowest part of the ditch alongside the road, if in fact there was a ditch at all. One of those times I looked back to see how Emerson was doing. I saw him put his rifle to his shoulder, to look at the sights I thought. The rifle went off! "An accident," I thought. No — he had shot at somebody! But he was shooting back into the woods behind us. "There's a German sniper in a tree over there!" said Emerson. I flattened out in the ditch and looked but didn't see anything. In a couple of minutes the "German sniper," we found out, was one of our own mortar men looking for an observation post. The mortar man was not hit but he certainly was scared. Emerson later told me he didn't think he would live through his first day in combat.

We spent a day or so in the town of Surré, where we outposted the town. Outside the house we occupied lay all kinds of equipment, G.I. and German both. The G.I. stuff probably had been dropped there during the first days of von Rundstedt's offensive when some of our boys were cornered there. The German stuff was dropped there only a few hours before when we recaptured the town. Looking over the discarded equipment, I found a nice aluminum canteen cup. Someone had picked up mine when we left Metz. Going into the house we were occupying, I asked one of the girls there for scouring powder. In no time I had the canteen cup gleaming. A lot of the discarded equipment had belonged to German paratroopers, which didn't do much for my morale.

That night I was picked to go on a ration-carrying detail. All I carried with me was my rifle. Hiking out to the farthest point that our jeeps could go, we picked up our loads and took off. I got stuck with a five gallon jerrican full of water. I slung my rifle diagonally across my back. Then I put a stake through the handles of the jerrican. I could now keep the jerrican on my back by holding on to the stake. In that way I covered over three miles going up and down some pretty steep snow-covered trails.

Occasionally the people in front of the column would find the going easier so they could go a little faster. Meantime the boys at the tail end of the column were still negotiating tough terrain. The result was those in back would lose contact with the boys in front. It was so dark we kept walking into trees even though we were attempting to hold on to the man in front. Whenever contact was broken, the leader of the column would find out only when someone with the front of the column realized there was no one following him. The leader would then have to retrace his steps to reestablish contact. After a couple of hours, we got the stuff up to the guys now on the front line.

When I got back to our platoon CP I met one of the guys in my squad who had come to carry a case of rations back to our squad. I helped him by carrying his rifle while he carried the rations. As we approached our house I saw the silhouettes of two German helmets looking at us from under an open shed. I pointed my rifle at the helmets, snapped the safety off and kept walking. I intended to empty the clip at the helmets if they moved.

Walking up to the shed with my heart in my mouth, I was finally able to make out what was holding the helmets up. I didn't know whether to be relieved or angry. There were bunches of straw under those two coal scuttle helmets. It was somebody's idea of a joke.

Battalion Headquarters wanted an ammunition report. We were going to make a dawn attack. That meant we would have to get up in time to turn in our bed rolls to the CP and hike up to the jumping-off point before dawn. We were up before four o'clock and on the road half an hour later. Just before we started moving

Lux gave us "The Big Picture." All he knew was that we had a big walk ahead of us, we attack at dawn and we were to follow the man in front. I recognized the country we were going through. I had been through there on the ration-carrying party.

When we got up to the jumping-off point, the column stopped moving and waited for dawn. I sat down in the snow, took my pack off and started to eat a cold K ration breakfast. I was almost finished eating when they passed the word back, "Heads up, we're moving!" I threw what was left of the ration away and started to put on my pack. We were on a steep slope so I appreciated the help I got from the fellow in back of me in getting my pack back on.

We moved over the top of the hill in a heavy mist just as the black was turning to grey. Going down the other side of the hill everything was extremely quiet. When we were almost to the bottom, it happened. A German machine gun started to send long bursts right through us. Lucky for me, the first bursts were aimed at some of the guys further forward.

When those white tracers came in my direction, I was hugging the snow as they cracked over my head. One of the guys started back up the hill crying, "I'm hit bad. I'm bleeding to death!" It was Whitman. He must have been the first one to come on that machine gun. This was the second time he had been hit and again he would be going back to the hospital. His total time in actual combat this time could be measured in minutes. Lt. Azbell yelled out loudly, "okay boys, get your grenades ready!" Whether he did that to make us feel better or to scare the Germans, I don't know. Then we started shooting. I'm sure most of the guys didn't know what they were shooting at. I could hardly see fifty yards into the mist.

As soon as Lt. Azbell made his reconnaissance, he must have concluded that we couldn't advance in that murderous fire. In a little while we pulled back slightly into a rather large depression in the hillside. The Company Headquarters group and the First Platoon, my platoon, started to dig in, in this long shallow depression.

Down in the forward end of this depression, Kibbler was shaking and digging like mad. He was Second Scout of the Second Squad and was right behind Lucas, the First Scout, when Lucas stepped on a mine. Lucas went sky high. They had been pretty good friends. The mine going off alerted the Germans and started them shooting. Bullets had plucked at Kibbler's pants and had gone through the raincoat on his belt. No one blamed him for the way he felt.

My partner, Joe, and McCarthy were sent to dig holes for themselves ten yards away from the right flank of the long depression. There they were to observe into a ditch that the Germans could use to sneak up on us. I immediately started digging my own hole but the ground was frozen and the going was slow.

Right next to me was an artillery Forward Observer calling in to headquarters on his radio. He would ask for a concentration of fire first here and then there. Sometimes he would get it and sometimes he wouldn't. He was a brand new Second Lieutenant and there were older Forward Observers with other attacking companies that wanted concentrations. The main reason he did not get what he asked for was that he couldn't observe the accuracy of his shooting. The woods were too thick and he couldn't see very far.

I was digging my hole very diligently when there was an ear-splitting explosion. I saw a column of black smoke reaching way up in the air right over the spot Joe was digging. It seemed impossible that Joe could have escaped being hurt in such a close hit. My stomach sank. After a minute or so, when it appeared likely there would be no follow-up shells, Joe came running over to my hole. He had his rifle in his left hand. I couldn't believe my eyes! The muzzle of his rifle was all shattered and bent, but he didn't seem to be hurt.

I asked Joe if he had been hit. He said no. He told me he had been bending over in his hole digging when the shell struck about five yards away. It knocked him down, but outside of a bruise on his right arm and a little shock, he was okay. Henley had collected a few pieces of shrapnel in his back and started back to the Aid Station immediately under his own power.

Killian, however, was in a bad way. The shell had landed about fifteen yards away and a fragment of shrapnel had gone through both cheeks of his behind. Lux was out there with him trying to tie him up. He couldn't do much to help because every one of the four wounds was bleeding profusely. In no time the bottom of his hole was red with blood. We sent back for litter bearers but they were having a busy time. Our own medic had gone back with Whitman.

In the beginning of the attack, Whitman and another man had gone out looking for the German machine gun, thinking to fire a rifle grenade at it. They had hardly gone any distance when the Germans spotted them and fired a burst. Whitman caught a slug in his arm that must have broken the bone. I saw him slide down into our ravine, his face white, clutching his upper arm, which seemed to be dangling. Doc immediately went to work on him. This caused Whitman to cry out in pain. After a couple of minutes when Whitman felt a little better, Doc helped him walk back to the Aid Station.

Joe started to dig in next to me. I noticed that he was digging with only one hand. He told me his right arm still hurt owing to the bruise. Then he asked me to put my hand down through the collar of his field jacket to the place that hurt to see if there was any blood. I put my hand in as far as it would go, perhaps not far enough. At any rate my hand came away clean. Joe went back to digging.

After a while Joe stopped digging again and I cut the sleeve of his field jacket open to just over the spot he complained hurt. Sure enough there was blood, though not very much. That was good enough for me. I told him to get the hell back to the Aid Station. Not Joe, he wasn't hurt bad enough! Later we found out the shrapnel had passed clear through his arm. Joe wanted to go on digging. I wouldn't let him. Finally he decided he was hurt badly enough. He stripped off all his gear and went back to the Aid Station. A little while later, after Joe left, I looked through his gear to see if there was anything I could use. Opening his pack, I pulled out an aluminum mess gear with a big hole in it.

Killian was still out there in his foxhole, which was not far from our ravine. We didn't want to leave him alone. However, there was no safe way for anybody to stay out there with him. We therefore decided to bring him in with us. With quite a bit of pain to Killian, we did this and set him down next to where I was digging. Poor Killian was too weak to even stir. He could only say a few words at a time in a low whisper. We placed him on an overcoat and covered him with another. Lux had cut away his pants and underwear in order to tie him up.

Lux worked on him a long time trying to stop the bleeding. He was only partially successful. After a while Lux came over to me crying, "I can't do anymore for him. He's dying!" Lux was only nineteen. He had seen guys killed before, but this was the first time he was feeling personally responsible for this man's survival. He asked me what to do next. I told him to finish digging his hole. It must have been over an hour before the litter bearers showed up and took Killian back. Later we heard conflicting reports that he had either died from loss of blood, or that he had survived.

When we found out that the shell that landed in our midst was made in the U.S.A., we didn't feel any better. It seemed that every time one of our own shells fell short, it would certainly get somebody. Could it be that our shells were far more potent than the Germans'?

That deadly German machine gun was silent for a long time so we suspected that it had been pulled back. The Germans sometimes did this after beating off our initial assault. Only a reconnaissance patrol could find out if it was still there. There were only four of us left in the platoon who were suitable for such a mission. They couldn't send the new guys and most of the old ones were either killed, hit, or in no condition for the job — Kibbler, for instance. That left Lux, Petrie, Heady and me. As we started off I thought that either we would not find that machine gun, or we wouldn't be coming back.

Heady, the father of five children, led the way. Next went Petrie followed by Lux and myself. We went down the very ravine that we thought the Germans might use to sneak up on us. We had only gone between one and two hundred yards when Heady saw something. We all came up to him to confirm what he saw. All I saw through the heavy underbrush was what must have been the head and shoulders of a German moving around about seventy yards in front of us. We pulled back and conferred in whispers. I maintained we had accomplished our mission, which was to establish whether or not that murderous machine gun was still there. The others agreed, so we went back and reported what we saw.

I am not sure whether they believed us, but that didn't bother me. It was only half an hour later that they wanted another patrol to see if the machine gun had been moved in the interim. We were the only ones to do the job. My heart sank. They told us to get ready again. Then it happened! The machine gun sent a burst in our direction. Happy day! That burst proved the gun was still there so we didn't have to go back to look.

All day long one of our boys out in front of us kept crying for help. He was hit badly and couldn't move. A litter squad went out to get him. The German machine gun fired on them too, pinning them down so that they couldn't move forward or back. Finally someone higher up decided we couldn't hold what we had taken, and that we would pull back. This would also give our artillery an opportunity to blast the area without fear of hitting our own people again.

The artillery threw in some white phosphorous smoke shells under cover of which we were supposed to retreat. However, we didn't get the signal to retreat until the smoke had cleared. Meanwhile, the litter squad which had been pinned down in front of us took advantage of the smoke to get the wounded guy back to our ravine. Here they took a few minutes' rest. The wounded man had been hit in the head and was delirious. Finally it came, "Get them on! We're moving back!" We went back to the town we came from, but not to the same house.

The next day they told us to get ready for a long hike. Naturally we thought that we were going back to the rear for a rest and reorganization. Sure enough we started toward the rear. We passed through a 105 MM artillery battery and then several 40 MM anti-aircraft guns. Soon we didn't hear any shooting. We changed direction several times. Then we started to hear artillery again.

When we heard a machine gun chugging away in the distance we knew we were not going back for a rest. We were merely shifting over to a new sector. Then I heard the rumble of tanks in the distance. Boy, what a German tank could do to us if it came on us on a road like this one. As the rumbling became more distinct, I became more nervous. I felt much better when we passed one of our tank destroyers sitting on the road.

At last we got to where we were going. We relieved another outfit and they moved out. Petrie and I shared one of their holes. It was still fairly light so we widened the hole and made a roof for it. We ripped some corrugated tin from a shed near our position. I pulled some fence posts out of the ground and used them as supports for the tin roof. We found a big cache of straw from which we got material for a mattress. On top of the tin roof we piled earth to stop shrapnel from tree bursts.

About twenty-five yards from us, a guy from the previous outfit lay dead in his hole. A shell had hit the tree next to his hole and rained shrapnel down on him. We were hoping they would pick him up before dark. They didn't.

With dusk we prepared for bed. We were pretty tired. Before going to sleep, I split with Petrie a can of fruit salad I got from home. I pulled guard from eleven to twelve o'clock. It was December 31, 1944, New Year's Eve. It was time to do some reminiscing. At midnight, I shook Petrie and told him, "Happy New Year. It's your turn for guard!" He got up and I crawled into the hole and went to sleep.

At one o'clock Petrie woke me up unintentionally when his guard was up and he crawled in beside me. At two o'clock they woke us all up to move to a town on top of a hill about a mile away where we were to dig in. They were expecting a counterattack in the morning. Just short of the town we picked up full size engineering picks and shovels. Ayers, who had taken over the platoon when Whitman was hit, showed us where to dig our hole. Petrie, Emerson and I were put together. We took our gear off and set to work. I got the pick and started swinging. After some minutes of hard work I had hardly chipped the frozen ground. I would have made more progress in concrete. It was a hopeless task.

We started looking for a place to stay in what remained of the shell-torn buildings. They were all practically leveled. Then Petrie found a soft spot right next to one of the buildings. We started digging. It went very fast. Evidently there had been some kind of hole there that had been filled with ashes. The ashes did not freeze. In a little more than an hour we had a fair size hole. I wanted to make a top for the hole but Petrie and Emerson wanted to go to sleep.

Next morning I got up to see beautiful sunshine. Air Corps weather! Sure enough, a couple of P-47s showed up in short order. Again and again they strafed the woods a couple of hills away. Then I could actually see bombs drop clear of the planes. Some planes dropped two bombs at a time. I think they must have been five hundred pound bombs. Some bombs went off right away. Some exploded after a short delay. And some didn't seem to go off at all. The planes must have discouraged the Germans because there was no counterattack that morning.

Surprise of surprises — hot chow for our New Year's breakfast! Half of us could go down to the little village in the valley where they were serving chow from large marmite thermos cans. I got a ladle of cereal, a couple of stewed prunes and a third of a cup of coffee, all very cold! I had no mess kit half so I borrowed one from Kibbler. After eating I started back to our hole to relieve Petrie so he could eat. On the way back I came to a little stream where I thought I could wash Kibbler's mess kit before returning it to him. I washed it out and waved it in the air to dry it. When I inspected it for cleanliness I found it was completely covered with ice. Rubbing it with dry sand was the only way I could get it clean.

In a couple of hours it was apparent there would be no counterattack. We were then pulled back into the small village, where we awaited marching orders. In the afternoon we started moving. We didn't reach our destination until after dark. Here we took over from another outfit at the edge of a pine forest. There was a shortage of holes. The orders were to have one man awake in every hole at all times. And so two men plus myself took over a two-man hole. We broke it down so one man was always outside the hole awake while the two other men slept.

In the morning we woke up to overcast skies. Sure enough this emboldened the Germans. They sent streaks of white tracers over our positions. I had been standing next to our hole when the shooting started, so I dived right into the hole on top of the other two men. They were sitting there making their breakfast. When the tracers let up a bit I folded my raincoat, put on my pack, generally got all my equipment together and got ready to move. I thought this was going to be a full-scale counterattack. With the situation potentially becoming fluid, I didn't want to risk leaving my raincoat if we had to move. However, soon the firing died out and all was quiet again. And so we settled down here to about ten days of foxhole life similar to our time in Gremercey Forest.

We fixed our hole up pretty nicely, widening it and smoothing out the bottom. We cut a stack of little sprigs of pine needles and spread them over the bottom of the hole. With the bed rolls we drew each evening, we were quite comfortable. To make things better, one of the new guys, Friedlander, moved out of our hole into another with Emerson. This allowed us to rearrange the guard roster so that we had one hour on and four off.

Of course, we weren't allowed to settle down so easily. One afternoon they sent us across the road where we were supposed to protect the flank. The ground was hard and we had trouble digging. A new man named Aires was now my partner. Together we dug the hole but didn't have time to put a top on it before dark.

There were only two of us in the hole and they wanted one man awake at all times. That way we could never get any rest in the full sense of the word. We compromised our safety by having one man sitting up for two hours listening. Lux came up during the night and was very disturbed at our arrangement. He took Aires to the hole he was occupying with Petrie. I went over to join Archie Campbell and Willie Zinnani. Now we had one hour on and two off which was more bearable, and we were able to do our guard duty properly.

The next day Aires and I did a really good job on our hole, putting a good stout top on it. Now we started a new guard arrangement with only one man awake for all three holes. That way we knew that someone was really awake at all times. That night had a tremendous barrage came in on us. In the morning we found the trees all around us scarred. Aires' equipment had holes in it. There was a large tree overhanging our hole and it no longer looked very stable. We dragged a huge limb across the top of our hole. This we felt would give us some protection should the tree come crashing down on us.

Every night the company kitchen sent up sandwiches: one large sandwich for each man. It wasn't much but it was a welcome relief from the now monotonous K rations. Then we got a load of packages from home. I got the usual well-rounded package containing all kinds of good things to eat. Some of the other guys weren't as lucky. They got such practical gifts as toilette sets and aftershave lotion.

We found a large stock of 88 MM shells close by. We had no use for the shells themselves but we were thankful for the methodical German mind that encased each shell in a beautiful wood box. We rolled the shells out of their boxes, broke the boxes up and used them for kindling. It was necessary not to allow the fire to get too large because the Germans had a nasty habit of dropping artillery shells on any smoke they could see.

One of our biggest nuisances was the way water in our canteens would freeze. In order to take a drink or if you wanted water to make coffee, you first had to heat the canteen to melt the ice. If you made the mistake of filling the canteen to the brim you would awake in the morning to find it distorted from its normal flat shape into an object as round as a beer bottle.

As long as we could build fires we could always get water by melting snow. I got about one sixth of a cup of water out of every full cup of snow that I melted over the fire. Of course the water we got that way was anything but clean. It had pieces of dirt, bark and pine needles floating around in it. However, it suited our purposes.

The cold had an unusual effect on my new partner, Aires. Every night he would urinate in his sleep. That put him in a terrible fix; namely, being wet in freezing weather. He had been an M.P. in South Carolina and had been frightened that he would get killed in one of the fights he had to break up. He therefore asked to be sent overseas. I told him to ask to be sent back to the Aid Station for treatment. He refused, saying they would accuse him of faking, and would not do anything for him anyway.

Henley finally got a break and was sent back with trench foot. Junior Hamilton disappeared on New Year's Eve, saying he was going to the Aid Station because he felt sick. The Aid Station had no record of him so we all assumed he had gone A.W.O.L., had deserted, or maybe had been captured. Months later he came back. He had been in the hospital with pneumonia. The Aid Station had neglected to make the proper record.

One morning we turned in our bed rolls early and got ready to launch an attack. Luckily for us, our platoon was in support. The Second and Third Platoons, being the assault platoons, pulled out ahead of us. Soon, we too began to move. We had gone only a few feet when the boys up front ran into a brick wall of opposition.

At this point I made my way to the closest foxhole. I got into the hole and waited for the time when we would move some more. We didn't move. Instead the Germans threw in a terrible barrage. Everybody dived for a hole. I crawled way back in the hole I was already in, and two guys joined me. In the hole we found a big box of pre-cooked cereal that we later made up with some powdered chocolate. It was quite a delicacy. We also found a bottle of aftershave lotion. I made one of the boys throw it out. I didn't like the idea of a shell fragment throwing glass splinters around.

In the afternoon, right after we had some incoming mail, a short, rotund guy by the name of Joe, a new man, suddenly dropped in on top of us. He didn't look very well. Then he told us what had happened. He was sharing a hole next to ours with "Pop" Burr who was a very congenial fellow, always with something funny to say. I liked him a lot. His nickname resulted from his inclination to remove his dentures which made him look like an old man. He was over thirty, comparatively old for this business. It seems Pop was standing up in their hole when a shell landed near them. A fragment cut through his throat. He was dead before he hit the ground. We couldn't blame Joe for not wanting to stay in such close quarters with Pop, who was not too pretty to look at.

About the same time, Mitchell, leader of the Second Squad, caught a couple of pieces of shrapnel. Before he left to get fixed up he made sure no one else in his squad got hit by the same shell that got him. We stayed there until after dark and then returned to the holes we originally occupied on the other side of the road. I was feeling pretty low and wanted to get into a hole and go to sleep. There was some confusion and we couldn't get settled very quickly.

While we were waiting, the shelling started again. This time a shell landed on the other side of a tree next to which I was standing. The tree absorbed the shrapnel, but the concussion knocked me down. My reaction was automatic. I just jumped into the nearest empty hole; got in as far as I could, and got ready to go to sleep. Later Lux came around and told us we would not have to stand guard. This made me feel better. Nevertheless, I crawled way back in the hole away from the entrance through which shrapnel might come. My level of fear was significant.

After a full night's sleep, my morale improved. Yesterday's attack had failed. Today we would try again. This time we would try to take that hill from a different direction. We hiked back and then parallel to the front line. Once again, we would assault that same hill that gave us so much trouble. In order to do so, we had to cross an open valley that was clearly visible from many hills the Germans still held. One by one we raced across about two hundred yards of snow-covered valley. Once on the other side, we started a long hard climb to reach the top of the hill. It was a slow process because there was no telling when we might run into a stream of tracers.

The climb was exhausting. Many times when I was overheated, with no sign of letting up, I pulled a spoon from my pocket, scooped up some snow, and ate it like ice cream. Friedlander, a new guy who was carrying the B.A.R., was having a lot of trouble dragging all that weight up the hillside. His face was getting more and more white. We finally got to the top without encountering any resistance. This was certainly different than the day before.

We went around to the other side of the hill and started to dig in. Friedlander dug about six inches when he fainted dead away. They brought him around in a few minutes, but he was too weak to keep digging or to walk back to the Aid Station. After a while, some litter bearers came to carry him back. Friedlander was thirty-two. He had suffered a heart attack.

That night Lux, Hansen and I dug in together. They told us the blankets wouldn't be up until late. Lux and Hansen decided to try going to sleep, using nothing but their two raincoats. They laid one raincoat on the ground and huddled together covering themselves with the other one. I chose to stand up in the hole and move around in order to get as much warmth as possible. I was willing to wait for the blankets. They lay there shivering for half an hour, and then decided I had the better idea.

Now one of them produced a can of dry heat. The flame from this heating unit gave off very little light so we decided to try heating a cup of coffee. I supplied the coffee powder and we all chipped in on the water. Hansen dug an additional depth in the bottom of our hole and put the dry heat can in it. Then while we covered him with a raincoat he lit the can and put the canteen cup with the water over the flame. When the coffee was ready, all three of us dipped into it with our spoons. After a while the coffee cooled off enough to drink it from the cup. What a grand and glorious feeling a swallow of hot coffee can give when you are very cold!

The blankets came after midnight. They had to be hand-carried over a long and tortuous route. We were lucky enough to get two bed rolls so that we could put a couple of blankets under us and the same number over us. I slept so soundly and comfortably that night that I did not wake up until the sun was out. And then I didn't feel like getting up. They wanted us to roll up the bed rolls so that we could be ready to move if we had to. Out in a field about half a mile away we watched a score or more Germans give up to a couple of G.I.s. They filed out of a large barn with their hands in the air.

Around noon we moved out to take the town of Lutremange. We didn't expect much trouble since Luke had led a four man patrol into the town and found no Germans. Nevertheless we approached the place carefully, ready for anything. We searched the town in record time. Before I knew it we had finished searching the town and picked out a house in which to stay. The house was dirty and in very poor condition. In an hour we had the house livable, so I went out to see what I could see. Lutremange had changed its appearance in an unbelievably short time. Just two hours earlier, the town was as quiet as a churchyard. Now trucks and men were moving in an unending stream through the town. Everywhere, G.I.s were working, salvaging the wrecks of buildings to make temporary homes for themselves.

There were civilians wandering around too. One civilian made straight for his cache of liquor hidden in a wood pile. He certainly was disappointed when he found all the bottles had been broken. I met him as he was taking his broken bottles with what was left of the contents back to his home. I struck up a conversation with him and he offered me a drink. Before I left him I was feeling pretty good, having sampled stuff from three of his bottles. He had an excellent bottle of cherry brandy that we emptied. I wandered on. In a few minutes I was glad I was high. There was a really gruesome corpse lying in a field. The body ended at the chest. More than half the face and skull were not there. All that remained was a shell of a man's face. There was a film of snow covering some of it.

At another place I saw six dead Germans stretched out side by side in all kinds of grotesque positions. They all had a dark brownish-green pallor which must have been brought on by the sub-freezing temperatures. The corpses I had seen in early autumn had yellowish-green complexions.

That night we relieved a platoon that was maintaining a roadblock about a mile up the road. There was very little shelter up there, and the previous platoon had not dug any holes so we got very cold. A couple of us were posted near a haystack so we investigated its housing potential. We were delightfully surprised to find that someone had burrowed out holes large enough for a man to creep into. We lost no time in doing just that. In a couple of minutes I was comparatively warm and comfortable. In the morning, a jeep came with hot chow for us. I got to the jeep a little late because there weren't enough mess kits for everyone. I had to wait until someone got through eating from his mess gear so I could use his. There was no way to wash the mess gear so I did without that formality. Right after breakfast we were relieved and went back to our abode in Lutremange.

After a couple of hours sleep I attended to my woefully neglected mail situation.

For the first time, I wrote home saying that I was seeing action. Up until then I was getting "excellent training." After the combat of the last months, I decided that it would be better to prepare the folks for bad news.

We were supposed to go out to the roadblock again at six o'clock. As we were getting ready to start, the order came down that the road block would no longer be required. We had been by-passed by some other unit and the front line was now two miles up the road. That sent my spirits sky high. A rest at last! Within a couple of days after we had kicked the Germans out of Lutremange, we were seeing good American movies there. We got hot chow for every meal and made French-fried potatoes between meals. In addition, P.X. candy rations came through along with some magazines. We were paid, this time in Belgian currency. There was only one guard post, which was only for one hour in front of Battalion Headquarters.

After the meager fare of K rations, all the rich food and P.X. candy affected me. When we went to get paid I wasn't feeling so good. While waiting my turn to get paid, I got worse. When I put my helmet down on the table so they could fill it with my pay, I was feeling so bad I paid no attention to how much I was getting. I just crammed the money into my pocket and staggered home. I barely made the doorway, sinking down on my bed roll which I didn't have the strength to unroll. Ayres, our current platoon sergeant, must have seen how I felt, and put someone else on guard in my place. The next morning, I got up feeling fit as ever.

On January 15th, I got a chance to take a shower. Those who were selected boarded trucks and took an inspiring, though cold, ride through the countryside. Everywhere you looked there were snow-covered fields surrounded by pine forests. Sometimes, when we were high on a hill, we could see for miles. Every once in a while I saw an entire small village nestled in a valley between two large hills. Naturally I appreciated the scenery more from the back of the truck than from on my own two tired feet. When we got to the showers, we found they had broken down and so we turned around and went back.

We were soon to leave the area of the "Battle of the Bulge," and with it, the extreme cold. Temperatures were so low that my feet, which would normally feel cold even in average cold weather, now hurt, a sure sign of approaching trench foot. The unusual cold was a constant preoccupation, complicating our primary concern for physical survival. Gloves were a basic necessity, yet we were constantly losing them because of our frequent movement. Once I saw a G.I. glove lying next to a tank destroyer that had been knocked out. Elated, I reached down to pick it up, only to discover a wrist protruding from it.

# 7 | ALSACE, HOLLAND AND GERMANY

On January 17, 1945 we climbed on trucks and were off again to Metz. It was still light when we got there. This time we got stuck in another ex–French, ex–German barracks. This one was made for ordinary infantry, and was consequently inferior. We were the first troops to use it since the German troops left. And so it fell to us to clean up the mess the Germans had left. I was put on a detail loading all kinds of refuse onto trucks. We then rode on these trucks through the city to some large shell craters.

The driver backed our truck up to a big bomb crater and we started unloading the stuff. All around us stood gaunt-faced Frenchmen of all ages, grabbing at whatever we threw over the side. Most of the stuff they couldn't use. But they took all articles of clothing. The luckiest of the bunch was a little boy who managed to catch a pair of shoes that my buddy threw to him. After we had thrown most of the junk off, a couple of the Frenchmen came up on the truck and finished the job.

The following day I rated a pass to town because I had been on the garbage detail the day before. We started off as a group of five G.I.s. Three of the group were only interested in one thing: women. Dutchik, a new guy, and I tagged along with the others for a while but finally broke with them in order to visit some ancient cathedrals. Two of the cathedrals were blocked off because they had been damaged by shell fire and were in a dangerous state of repair.

The largest cathedral was open to the public but in a sad state. Most of the windows were boarded up. Many of the stained glass windows were blown out. This resulted in the entire floor and all the seats being covered with a blanket of snow. The uncovered windows that remained were really beautiful, being full of strong colors and very finely made. The high ceiling, tall pillars and symmetry of the architecture were inspiring as you walked down the long center aisle.

After about five days we were off again. The Germans were counter-attacking in the south. This time we went to the Vosges Mountains, which were in the Seventh Army sector. Up until now we had been in General Patton's Third Army. The exact location was the Dominale Forest not far from the fortress town of Bitche in Alsace, France. The large city in the area was Colmar. Late in the afternoon we detrucked in a small Alsatian town where we waited for dark to hike the last couple of miles to the front line. The town was a peculiar sight. It must have changed hands several times. Each time the conqueror would string up his own communication wire, so now there was such a maze of wire hanging all over the place that the boys had a good laugh.

We spent a good part of time in the town waiting in a broken barn around small fires. Towards evening the people who owned the barn started to worry that we might accidentally burn down what remained of the barn with our small fires. They got patriotic and invited us into their home where we could keep warm without building dangerous fires on their property. Everybody relaxed as well as they could, trying to get as much rest as possible. At 9:00 p.m. I went out to relieve Archie Campbell who was standing local security guard right outside the door. At 9:30 the order came: "Get 'em on!" I went inside and got my equipment. In a few minutes we were on the road on the way up to the front.

It took over two hours for us to negotiate the four miles of snow-bound road. Officially we were relieving the 100th Division at midnight. At 11:45 we got to where we were going, the clothes sticking to my back with sweat. Immediately another guy and I went out to the outpost to relieve the 100th Division men who were manning it. They had a machine gun out there which they took with them. We couldn't get hold of our weapons platoon right away so we dragged two B.A.R.s out there to replace the machine gun. From midnight until two o'clock the two of us stood around clapping our hands and stamping our feet to keep the sweat from freezing on us. When our relief showed up we went back about one hundred yards to the cellar we would call home for the next week or more.

What a surprise I got when I walked into the First Squad's room! There were mattresses all over the floor and a warm stove in the corner. Lux had reserved a place for me next to him on a large double mattress. What luxury! I could take my snow-pack boots off and dry their felt inlays and my socks on the stove while I slept on a comparatively soft mattress. They woke me up a little before eight so that I could go out on the eight to ten shift. The guard was arranged on a two hours on and four hours off basis. That's the way it went straight through, day and night for about ten days.

My average schedule was to sleep from 8 a.m. to midnight, go on guard from midnight to 2 a.m., sleep from 2 a.m. to 6 a.m., then go on guard from 6 a.m. to 8 a.m. Breakfast was eaten from 8 a.m. until noon. I then went on guard duty until 2 p.m., followed by dinner and writing letters. Although it was bitterly cold and the snow blew in our faces while on guard, we considered ours a good deal. We could sleep comfortably and get dry whenever we got wet, and we were getting hot chow.

They finally put a 50 caliber machine gun in our outpost. That didn't make me particularly happy because our fifties were not very reliable. They were usually mounted on the company jeeps, went through all kinds of weather and got very little attention from the jeep drivers. Our outpost was in a field about fifty yards away from the nearest house, which was at the edge of a small village. They put a field phone in the outpost so we could call the platoon CP where we slept. In front of the outpost stretched a large rolling field. On the other side of the field, about a mile away, stood a pine forest occupied by the Germans.

The building closest to our outpost housed some of the boys who manned an outpost at a window on the second floor. In the cellar of that house there were five divisional engineers living very comfortable lives. Their only job was to set off a charge of dynamite under a nearby bridge, if and when the order ever came through. There was also a 57 MM anti-tank gun very cleverly camouflaged standing right in front of the building. The crew manning that gun had another room in the same building. They also had a machine gun set up pointing out of a window. This building was across the road, directly opposite our house.

After a couple of days the monotony began to tell on us. We got two more replacements for the First Squad. Goodwin was one and Kearns the other. Goodwin was a little nervous and talked a great deal. He was accepted into the group quickly. Kearns was quiet and seemed somewhat bewildered by it all. Campbell and Emerson had the job of running contact patrols to another company about a thousand yards down the road in a neck of woods. Campbell managed to get a regulation white camouflage coat. Emerson had to content himself with a white bed sheet. With white snow covering everything, whatever we could do to blend into the background became very important. At first I just secured a piece of white lace over my helmet. Later I found a white bed sheet that fit me nicely after I cut a hole in it for my head, and knotted up some loose ends.

One night, about four in the morning, I heard Emerson and Campbell wondering whether it was time for them to start on their connecting patrol. Campbell, who had more experience, decided they would wait a little longer. Just then a burst of German "burp" gun fire rattled off the bricks of our building. I got up and gave Lux a poke. He was a heavy sleeper and took quite a bit of waking. When he finally realized the situation he took off to where Lt. Shoptease, our new platoon leader, was talking to Luke at the outpost. He returned in a minute with the news that the outpost was surrounded.

The outpost not being more than a hundred yards away, it meant the Germans were virtually on our doorstep. My heart sank to my boots and lower. We all started to get our equipment on in a hurry. I was so frightened and flustered that I could hardly buckle on my belt. I was literally shaking. Any second I expected the explosion of a grenade in the corridor. By this time the gunfire had really started up in earnest. Our boys across the street were answering with a large volume of fire. Their building gave them direct observation of the Germans in the field, while ours did not.

We got out in the snow and set up a defensive ring around our building. The guys across the street continued sending a continuous stream of hot lead at the Germans. I could see the red flashes of their M-1 Garand rifles as they fired through a breach in the wall of their wrecked building. The flashing was almost continuous. There wasn't room enough for more than ten guys to be firing at one time and yet their firepower was terrifying. As soon as I got outside, I felt better. At least now I could see for a little distance all around me. I knew I could shoot any German before he came within hand grenade-throwing distance.

Off in the distance I heard some German yelling orders. Our own lieutenant, Shoptease, an American Indian, was strutting around bolt upright giving orders in a loud voice. As far as I was concerned, he was taking an unnecessary risk, but it was apparent he knew what he was doing. I was glad we had him in command rather than some other officer in the company. After twenty minutes of continuous firing there was no answering fire, so Shoptease gave the cease fire order. Everything was still. We hadn't really expected to defend the place against such a large scale attack, so we hadn't dug any holes around the building. This we rectified immediately by digging the necessary holes. I started to dig into the soft snow that filled a ditch alongside the road. Now it was getting light fast. About then I heard the anti-tank gun squad throw a shell into the breach of their gun. They hadn't fired that big gun or even their light machine gun. As far as the engineers went, I don't think they ever bothered getting out of bed. Our big fifty-caliber machine gun had refused to fire. The action was frozen by the cold and possibly dirt. After daylight came, they managed to get it talking. Our whole defense had been taken up by the M-1's.

When the sun started to shine, we captured a prisoner. In the dark one of the German medics had covered himself with snow. When daylight came he took out some white bandages and waved them back and forth as a sign of surrender. We yelled and motioned for him to come in. After considerable coaxing, he finally did so.

Shoptease knew I could speak a little German so he asked me to question him. He said there were forty men in the attacking force and that we had hit three of them and driven off the rest. Their mission, he said, was to take and hold the two houses we were in. Probably, had they been successful, a larger attack would have been launched to capture the entire village. I took his belt as a souvenir and went back to digging.

Before noon we were told to stop digging and leave the holes as they were. That evening they told us that we would be relieved by another division. Happy day! I don't think I could have been at ease in that place anymore. I was on guard at the outpost when the relieving division arrived. Our outpost was the last to be relieved so we had to hustle to get our stuff on and move out with the company. When I caught up to the company I was handed a package from home that had just arrived.

We were going back to the same town we detrucked in over a week before. The walk back was just as bad as the one coming in only more so. A lot of snow had fallen since then. Fortunately someone had reserved a house for us, so we got right in out of the weather. Once in the house I threw my rifle and pack into a baby's crib to reserve it for myself to sleep in. Then I opened the package, the contents of which the boys and I finished off in short order. Instead of staying there for the night we were loaded on trucks and taken for a two hour ride. We got off the trucks and stood around freezing for about half an hour while the mayor of this little Alsatian village ran around looking for a place for us to sleep. He finally got us into a combination tavern and general store.

Goodwin and I put our bed rolls down together in a hallway and went to sleep. We were supposed to move out again at dawn, so as soon as it started to get light we rolled up our bed rolls and made and ate our breakfast. We ate in a hurry so as to finish before the order to move out came. After eating we sat down on our bed rolls and started to wait. We waited one hour, two, three and then finally formed up on the road at noon. While waiting for our trucks we watched an armored outfit being fed hot chow. Not being the bashful type, I got into their chow line. I got myself a great big slab of bread piled high with hot meat and a cup of hot coffee. I had been working on my open sandwich about five minutes when our trucks pulled up. It almost broke my heart to have to throw away what I hadn't had time to eat.

It was only a short ride to a railroad marshaling yard. We immediately boarded a "40 Hommes 8 Cheveaux" box car. We also took on enough rations for three days. Instead of starting right off as we expected, we were allowed to get off and run through a Red Cross Clubmobile. While we got our doughnuts and coffee, the girls played some real American music and danced with some of the guys. When it started to snow, the dancers retired to an empty box car and continued to dance. Naturally I went through the line several times, mostly to build up my doughnut reserve.

About four o'clock, we moved out in a heavy snow storm. Things would have been cramped even without all the equipment we were carrying. I hooked the sling of my rifle around some of the braces in the roof. My pack and cartridge belt I hooked on to an iron ring on the wall of the box car. I shoved my bed roll against the wall so I could sit on it. The other twenty or so guys handled their equipment in like manner. Wherever you looked things were swinging and bumping your head when you stood up.

It hardly started to get dark when some of the boys opened their bed rolls and spread them on the floor. They weren't taking any chances on not getting sufficient room to stretch out. Lux and I were sleeping next to each other so we didn't waste any time following the early bird's example. Things were tight indeed when everybody lay down to sleep. Lux's and my feet were tangled up with the feet of the guys sleeping opposite us. During the night my feet started to hurt because of the constant weight of other feet on top of them. I had the devil's own time trying to extricate them. And when I finally accomplished my mission, I couldn't find a place to put them down. This went on for three days.

We passed through several large French cities heading north. Then I noticed a sign on a building: "Belgie." We were back in Belgium. This time we saw the industrial part of the country. There were many large factories very reminiscent of northern New Jersey. Now we changed direction. We were no longer headed north. We were going east toward the front. The train slowed down as we passed through the city of Liege. The population waved to us. I thought they might well wave to us; some of us on the train were going to get killed protecting them.

Another thought, although only a momentary one, was that as long as we were riding around from one front to another we were not on the line and getting shot at. On the outskirts of Liege the train ground to a halt to take on water. A woman with her little boy came out of a house. The child had a wide ribbon with the Belgian national colors — black, orange and yellow — which he gave to one of the G.I.s on the train.

We finally got off the train on the third day. We were taken by truck to a very tidy little village. Lt. Feeney gave us a little speech after we detrucked. He said the population here was Dutch and were very friendly and we were not to do anything to change it. Then we waited around while they found places for us to stay. There was a girl hanging out of a window watching us. Walking up to her, I asked in French, "Parlez vous Francais ici?" She looked at me quizzically and said in English, "What did you say?" That shut me up but good.

My platoon got a raw deal in that we were the last to be housed. The other platoons managed to get very nice quarters. The only housing left when we got there were barns. Nevertheless, we were treated royally. The farmer whose barn we were in cleaned it out thoroughly and gave us fresh straw to sleep on. While we couldn't sleep in the house because it was already filled with members of our weapons platoon, we could spend our days there. The most important attraction in this farm house was its electricity and consequent radio. The Allied Expeditionary Force radio network broadcast all the best American records.

We naturally showed our appreciation for being treated so nicely by giving the Dutch farmer chocolate and cigarettes. They hadn't tasted chocolate in Holland for four years. That night while we were getting ready for bed the farmer came around with a big steaming pot of hot chocolate his wife made up from the chocolate we had given him earlier. On the second night, army personnel started giving motion picture shows in a big barn down the road. On our way there we asked any and all civilians to join us at the movie. We had half the children of the village with us. The people were so friendly you couldn't pass them without getting a "Hello!" After two days the G.I.s were saying hello to each other out of habit.

After several days they asked for an ammunition report and we got ready to move. We were certainly unhappy when we put on our equipment and started toward the road. As we passed the farmhouse, each one of us shook hands with the genial Dutch farmer. The whole population came out to see us leave. Everyone waved as our trucks roared out of the village.

Before we knew it we had crossed back into Germany. The German towns were pretty well torn up. We detrucked in a large town called Heinesberg. We immediately formed up and moved up to the front. As we were going up we met units of the British brigade we were relieving going the other way. Like all infantrymen, they weren't the neatest people but they did seem happy we were relieving them. After about four kilometers we came into a village the outskirts of which would be our front line. Its name was Kirchoven.

We took over a house from one of the British platoons. When we got there the British had a patrol out so they had to wait for them to return before they could leave. Out in the street was a six pounder anti-tank gun, the forerunner to our 57 MM anti-tank gun. Unlike the way we used our anti-tank guns, the British brought theirs up to the front line. I talked to the gun crew for a while. They had actually seen a lot of action against tanks whereas our anti-tank crews seem to have seen little action. As far as I knew, their guns could have been used mainly to protect CPs in the rear.

The guys we were relieving had taken the town less than a week before. The thing that struck me most about these British infantrymen was their similarity to us in the way they did things. Many of them were very young, about eighteen. The British had a Bren machine gun pointing out of a window of our new house, so we replaced it with one of our machine guns. As a bonus to our squad, we were able to get the machine gun squad to share our guard duties. We also had to maintain a road block of mines laid across the road at night.

When we walked into the house we found it clean and warm. The British had left the fire in the stove burning. There were a few mattresses there, but the first guys in had claimed them. The rest of us, myself included, had nothing on which to sleep. In talking to the English anti-tank boys, I found out some of them had been living in an air raid shelter nearby and they had left lots of mattresses there. I got one of our guys to accompany me and went down there to investigate. Not only did we find all the mattresses we needed, but also a sealed tin of English biscuits. While these biscuits weren't as good as those in K rations, we ate them to relieve the monotony. The British probably left them because they couldn't stomach them anymore.

Altogether there were supposed to be four men on guard at all times during the night. Two of the men were posted in a foxhole in the backyard of the house. After we saw how quiet it was we cut this post to one man — without the knowledge of the platoon leader. There was supposed to be one man each on the machine gun and the front door. After a few days we let the man on the front door handle the machine gun too, again without the platoon leader knowing it.

To our squad also fell the task of running two contact patrols each night with another battalion. They were holding the other side of town. On about the second day we gathered up four very serviceable bicycles, which cut the thirty minute patrol down to a very stimulating five minutes. Of course no one knew we used bicycles. We just left them outside when we went into the other battalion's CP to report. It would have been very uncomfortable for us if some German patrol had decided to contest our right of way on that road. We rationalized our laziness by saying it is very hard to hit a moving target, especially in the dark. Of course all these labor-saving schemes added to our sleeping time. No one guy had to put in more than one or two hours a night on guard.

One night, at about two o'clock, Lt. Feeney, to whose platoon we had been attached, came rushing in with the news that there was a heavily armed ten man German patrol loose in the town, and one of the Germans could speak perfect

**The real faces of war: Mosher, Hansen. Terry. March 6, 1945 — RHINEBERG. Here I got my first camera and started taking pictures.**

English. Then he looked to see if the guard was properly posted. Willie Zinnani, who had been standing at the door when Feeney came in, now ran to the machine gun. Feeney, seeing the machine gun manned, now went out back to see if the prescribed two men were there. Finding only one, he started back only to bump into one of our boys going toward the backyard. This guy told Feeney he had just gone to the house to wake up their relief. In reality, Zinnani had sent him there with that story.

Whether Feeney was entirely taken in or not, we didn't know but he didn't say anything. Two hours later, after everyone had been awakened and gotten their equipment ready for action, we found out that the so-called English speaking German patrol was in fact a patrol from Company A that had gotten lost.

Just as darkness fell every evening, we laid a mine field of English land mines across the road in front of our house. For twenty feet on each side of the mine field we put up a light wood and barbed wire barrier to serve as a warning to any of our

We slept below the beer hall in the background. There we found a barrel of beer which we finished before we left.

**The first picture of me in Europe.**

own vehicles that might accidentally come up this road. The man posted at the front door served as an additional warning mechanism for our vehicles. One night while I was on the front door guard post I heard a vehicle coming my way. I stepped out of the doorway and prepared to yell, "Halt!" to the driver. I got nervous when I realized how fast he was coming.

I yelled, "Halt!" three or more times as loud as I could. The driver didn't hear me. I heard the vehicle crash through the barrier. I dived for the doorway amid a prolonged screech of brakes. Then silence. Then cursing!

I got up slowly and walked over to see two guys sitting in a jeep with the barricade hanging in shreds from the back of the vehicle. They were angry because someone had left an obstacle in the road. I made them get out and look at the English mine that one of the wheels had pushed along in front of it. If the wheel hadn't been locked by the brakes, it would have rolled over the mine. Instead the locked wheel had pushed it along. They weren't angry anymore. They were busy sweating. After that, at my suggestion, we doubled the distance of the barricades from the mines.

*    *    *

At this point in recording the preceding events, my 70 day furlough came to an end. I put down my pencil and went to Fort Dix to be discharged. I did not look at these notes again for fifty-seven years.

It is in February of 1945 that this narrative is interrupted. However, I was able to continue the story with the aid of photos I took with a camera I obtained while still in combat in March of 1945.

I have yet to learn of any front line infantryman (rifleman) taking photos in combat; that is, seeing a battle in which he is personally engaged, not as an observer, as in the case of Signal Corps photographers, but as an active individual participant.

# 8 | Co. E Takes Ossenberg

**March 8, 1945 — OSSENBERG — We attacked this village at dawn. Ossenberg is on the west side of the Rhine River which we were soon to cross.**

Advancing against small arms fire we ducked into a nearby house. A tank from the 784th Tank Battalion (a black unit) pulled up to help us. I pointed out the direction the enemy fire was coming from and the tank opened fire on it.

After the tankers threw out the empty ammunition belts and boxes and spent car-tridge cases that were cluttering up their tank, they moved around the side of our house. From this new position they were better able to see all the houses we were getting fire from and to return that fire.

This photograph shows the spot the tank just left. Everything is all ground up, including the ornamental iron fence. The tank left an unmistakable footprint.

The tank is now in its new firing position and is returning the enemy's fire. Through the haze of the gun smoke you can see one of the buildings from which we were receiving fire.

Our house has been hit by artillery which tore a hole in the side of the building through which I was able to take this picture.

March 9, 1945 — The night before we moved up a couple of houses and held for the night.

At dawn we received a terrific artillery barrage. For several minutes there was a constant screaming and exploding of shells.

Under cover of this very heavy fire, the Germans were able to roll an 88 MM gun out into the open and deliver direct fire on all visible targets. It was thus that they were able to hit this tank and our CP with such accuracy.

March 10, 1945 — This is a self-timed picture with the camera on the ground.

The tank is still smoldering. Two 88 MM shell holes are visible in the tank, one in front of my head and the other behind my shoulder.

There are still two bodies in the lower front part of the tank. They were taken out the next day, shapeless, blackened masses. This is something I did not want to remember.

This photograph is also self timed, meaning I set up the camera so that the shutter release would go off after I got into the picture. It was taken from the same spot as the previous photograph, except that the camera is pointed more to the right.

The picture shows our company CP with the bed rolls out in front. It was probably hit by the same 88 that got the tank.

The first round hit above the doorway. It was followed by two more rounds that went right through the doorway. In the foreground lies a calf that was run over by a tank.

The camera's self-timer went off just as I saw the interior in the next picture.

This photograph shows the interior of the Company CP where we had eight casualties. Kap Keplinger, who helped me dig my first foxhole, was killed. Ray Lux was one of the wounded. He wouldn't return to the outfit for many months.

Everything shown in the picture is covered in plaster dust.

Leaning against some of the wreckage is a dismembered leg. Shredded trousers are hanging from it.

At this time back home it might have seemed that the war was winding down. Not so for us.

Another self-timed picture with the camera on a fence post. With my left hand, I am pointing to a shell hole that was made at dawn the day before, during that terrific barrage.

Vernon Kearns and I were asleep inside this house when one of the shells made the hole I'm pointing out.

We were showered with glass and plaster but were not hurt.

Several of the previous pictures were taken from around a corner of the house.

The shell that hit here tore off a piece of the wagon wheel at left and broke many of the tile shingles of the roof.

March 11, 1945 — The front line has passed us by. It has moved forward enough so that it is safe to walk around.

As we were fighting our way into Ossenberg, this German soldier, probably a scout, was observing us from a rise of ground a couple of hundred yards away.

Kibbler, who was a rifle shooting enthusiast as a civilian, saw and shot this German.

As the picture shows, Kibbler hit him squarely in the center of his helmet.

After being hit, the soldier slid down the embankment. He was out of sight and laid there undisturbed until Kibbler, the only one who knew he was there, led us to him.

In the foreground lies a photograph of this German as he looked as a civilian.

What a waste!

*Left:* "Blackie," a jolly guy from the hills of Arkansas. On one patrol he put down his M-1 rifle in favor of a double barreled shotgun he found in a farmhouse. He was fond of automatic pencils, of which he has several in his shirt pocket. Here he is in front of the window under which we were sleeping when that shell exploded. *Above:* Kibbler, who shot the German on the previous page, has just had a drink of schnapps he and Blackie found. It was a way of putting the days before and ahead out of your mind.

# 9 | ACROSS THE RHINE

The capture of Ossenberg brought us up to the west side of the Rhine River. The Rhine River now became a major defensive position for the German army. At this point, all the Allied armies were making ready to force a crossing of this real and symbolic barrier. During the lull, the 35th Division was in reserve, getting ready for the battle on the other side of the Rhine. March 16–25, *[continued on p. 90]*

Emerson in front of a "Wermacht" truck with the slogan in German reading, "Where we stand, stands (the border of) Germany!"

*[continued]* 1945 — Our battalion is in a village 40 kilometers west of the Rhine. This is E Company's first parade in Europe. 1. Watson 2. Kibbler 3. Zinnani 4. Campbell 5. Lasley 6. Stelling 7. Rockwell 8. Friedman 9. Cross.

Emerson is posing for another picture to be sent home. He is wearing a wool hood his wife had knitted for him.

Like everyone else I want a picture to send home. I am carrying a carbine instead of an M-1, since I am now part of a Bazooka team.

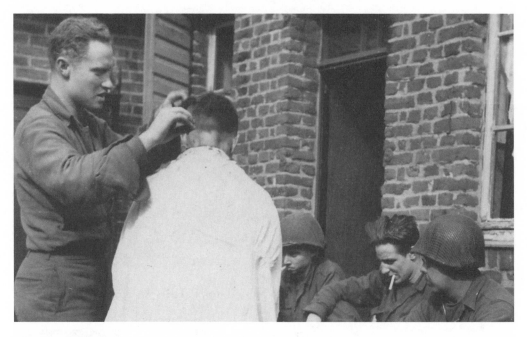

"Red" Nova is the self-appointed company barber. I traded this picture for a haircut. Red had just returned from the hospital after being hit by shrapnel while taking a shower near Rhineberg.

I am practicing with a 60 MM mortar as part of a program to teach everyone to use another weapon in case of concentrated casualties.

*Above:* March 26, 1945 — We crossed the Rhine River on a pontoon bridge about a mile from Rhineberg. Two days earlier they had told us the 30th and 79th Divisions were forcing a bridgehead across the Rhine. On "D" plus 3 (March 27) we were to pass through these divisions and act as a spearhead for the drive.

*Right:* We are just starting across on the pontoon bridge. We are about halfway across. A smokescreen obscures the river bank.

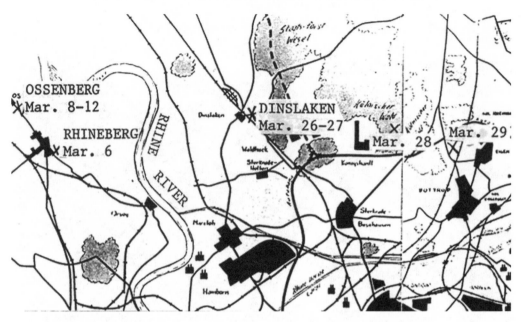

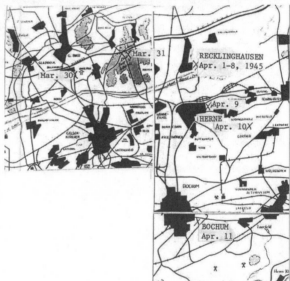

***This page and facing:*** March 26, 1945 — Dinslaken — The vacation is over! This is our staging area for an attack to begin the next morning. While here I look the town over.

*Above:* March 27, 1945 — A few miles east of Dinslaken. We attacked in the morning but did not get very far before an automatic 20 MM cannon pinned us down. Above, my squad is taking cover in a water-filled ditch.

*Left:* This was taken shortly after the one above. I was standing up to get a better angle when I heard a shell coming in. On my way down I clicked the shutter, which accounts for the blurring. Note the first man now has his head buried in the mud while his feet are deep in the water.

This photograph was taken from the same spot except it shows the other side of the same ditch. Kearns, with his feet also in the water, has closed his eyes waiting for our next move.

After moving back a few hundred yards we started to dig in. Here Cross, who is digging next to me, stops to eat some chocolate.

The tanks showed up in the afternoon, shooting up everything in sight. We followed them soon afterwards.

*This page:* Men, women and children of all ages take part in Hitler's Total War!

*Opposite, bottom:* March 28, 1945 — East of Dinslaken. German refugees pass us while we are in reserve.

March 29, 1945 — East of Dinslaken. *Top:* A German roadblock, half of which lies in its cradle unused while the other half has been pushed aside by a tank. *Bottom:* Freshly captured and still haughty Nazi officers.

Zinnani is right in front of me. Just beyond the overpass is a knocked out U.S. tank.

March 30, 1945 — We entered the town of Eigen. Everything is quiet.

Blackie is talking to Rockwell during the quiet capture of the town. A few minutes later, a sniper fired and everyone disappeared.

March 30, 1945 — East of Bottrop — The Air Corps got here before us! Kearns, my partner, carrying the folded bazooka, is walking alongside Blackie while I stop to take this picture.

Leaving Bottrop, Rockwell is in front.

Before entering Bottrop I saw a direct hit on the onion shaped tower.

*Opposite, bottom:* East of Bottrop — Blackie, in the foreground, is going up hill.

We move up while German P.O.W.s move to the rear.

Howard Ayres watches me take a shot of German P.O.W.s. The next week a German bullet shattered his leg.

*Opposite, bottom:* March 30, 1945 — This is a housing complex east of Bottrop. We liberated these French slave-laborers just a few minutes before. We had attacked this place riding on tanks. Campbell and I got off our tank and were sent to check out this basement. When I realized the people we found here were French, I yelled out, "Viva la France!" at which they nearly tore us apart.

March 31, 1945 — East of Bottrop, a very narrow road, just enough room for one tank.

The Autobahn — After walking on this super-highway a short distance, we turned off.

Kearns, resting, holds his carbine and watches the tanks roll by.

April 1, 1945 — We walked into Recklinghausen.

I ran across the street to take Watson's picture. "Doc," our medic, turned around.

Lasley watched me take this picture.

Zinnani and Rockwell passed in front of one of the city's few wrecked buildings.

These apartment houses overlooked the Emscher Canal, where we spent a week on the front line encircling the Ruhr Pocket.

# 10 | THE RUHR POCKET

The part of Germany known as the Ruhr is a heavily industrialized area. About this time we had almost surrounded the Ruhr.

April 8, 1945 — RECKLINGHAUSEN — Near midnight I went on guard, out-posting a heavy machine gun platoon. It had as its mission the delivery of "harass-ing" fire on the Germans who were in Herne, just across the Emscher Canal in the Ruhr. The photo shows the tracers of four machine guns reaching into Herne, set-ting two houses afire.

At four o'clock that night we moved right up to the canal. At daybreak, Kearns and I were sent back to guide vehicles with assault boats to our position.

April 9, 1945 — We were at the Emscher Canal. Instead of using the assault boats, we walked along the canal until we came to a set of blown-up locks.

April 9, 1945 — In a garage in Herne a Signal Corps photographer prepares to take the semi-posed picture shown on the next page.

*Opposite:* April 9, 1945 — Emscher Canal — A double exposure! I forgot to wind the film. It shows Emerson across, Cross in the middle and Cooper about to cross on a 4 × 6 wooden plank.

Richards is holding his B.A.R. Moss is holding a "walkie-talkie." Another man is looking out the door — all posing! Only one man in back is looking for the enemy through a window.

April 9, 1945 — HERNE — After crossing the canal and a dry stream bed, we stopped for a breath. In the picture above, we started again. The man in front of me has just started to run for the factory in the distance.

While I am covering one of the entrances to the above factory, Ayres came running towards me. Just as he reached the entrance there was a burst of machine gun fire, and Ayres tumbled through the door. He had been hit! The bullet had broken a bone in his leg. I immobilized the leg with the help of some flexible notebooks. Some time later, when the litter bearers were taking him away, he gave me his trench knife, which I still have.

In this same factory, Richards was hit in the head. This gave me quite a scare because he seemed to be bleeding from both sides of his head. Could the bullet have gone through? Fortunately, both wounds proved to be superficial.

Before nightfall we reached our objective: the railroad track that bisects the city.

April 10, 1945 — HERNE — At dawn we resumed the attack. Here the man in front of me is about to run under the railroad bridge on the right.

*Opposite:* We are attacking in the early morning fog with tank support. Kearns, my partner, is in front of me with our bazooka.

In the thick early morning haze, Garvey has hurt his hand and Doc fixes him up, while Dutchik kneels in front, playing it safe.

April 10, 1945 — HERNE — The cry goes up, "Tank dozer forward!" There's a road block up ahead that needs flattening.

We watch as the tank dozer tears through the road block.

April 10, 1945 — South of Herne — Zinnani watches German civilians plant a white flag in their front yard. A few minutes before, when they first saw us, they shook hands with each other, congratulating themselves on having lived through the war.

April 11, 1945 — WANNE-EICKEL — We entered without resistance.

April 11, 1945 — En route from Wanne-Eickel (8 km back) to Bochum (10 km ahead). Polly believes in being prepared, hence a full cartridge belt plus three bandoliers of rifle ammunition.

We finally got to Bochum with tired feet, but no one shot at us.

*Top and above:* April 11, 1945 — BOCHUM — The population comes out of a four story concrete air raid shelter to watch us take over.

All the military personnel left in the city wait for us in front of their City Hall.

*Right:* Everything we needed to live and fight had to be on us at all times. On my belt are two 15 round magazines for my carbine. To the right of the magazines is a folded shovel in its carrier. Also on the belt, but not visible, are a first aid kit, a water-filled canteen, and in back, a folded raincoat.

I'm wearing a field jacket with two huge pockets in front. True, you could put K rations in those pockets. However, this would interfere with hugging the ground as closely as possible when we had incoming mail. Hooked through a ring on my harness is the handle of a hand grenade. For safety I put tape around the grenade's activating ring.

Looking for targets.

*Opposite, bottom:* **April 12, 1945 — South of Bochum — A tank destroyer fires its 90 MM gun across the Ruhr River into what's left of the Ruhr Pocket. The picture was taken from the window of the house we slept in. Note the size of the empty shell cases.**

April 12, 1945 — South of Bochum — These photos were taken from the turret of the tank destroyer on the previous page.

Our artillery shells can be seen exploding on the other side of the Ruhr River. The river is the white streak near the right edge of the pictures.

*Opposite, bottom:* The tank destroyer men are searching for targets to engage.

# 11 | THE FINAL DAYS

Here we recrossed the Emscher Canal to bypass the Ruhr Pocket and head deeper into Germany.

*Opposite:* As the Ruhr Pocket was collapsing at an ever increasing rate, we were pulled out of the line. Our new mission was to make a dash to the east, to the Elbe River, as part of a Combat Team. The Russians were coming from the east. We would meet them at the Elbe.

April 13, 1945 — HERNE — We returned here to be loaded on trucks. Now we were on our way back along the same route we had taken getting here in four days of attacking. We had actually fought along this very street.

East of the Weser River — The Second Armored Division is spear-heading the drive. Consequently, we rolled right along.

*Opposite, top:* April 13, 1945 — We're on the highway east of Recklinghausen. Near here we ran into an ambush that cost three of the enemy their lives. We saw them first!

   *Opposite, bottom:* The WESER River — Our truck is almost across this pontoon bridge. The rest of the convoy is waiting its turn on the far bank.

April 13, 1945 — East of the Weser River — After riding all day for a total of 220 miles, we stopped here for the night.

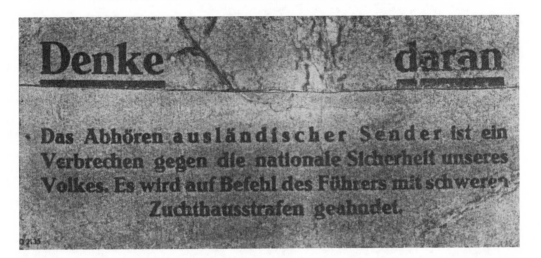

# THINK      ABOUT IT

The listening to foreign radio is a crime against the National security of our people. It is an order of the Fuehrer with heavy prison penalties.

*Top and above:* I found this notice stuck on the same radio on which we heard that President Roosevelt had died. Below is my best effort at translating it.

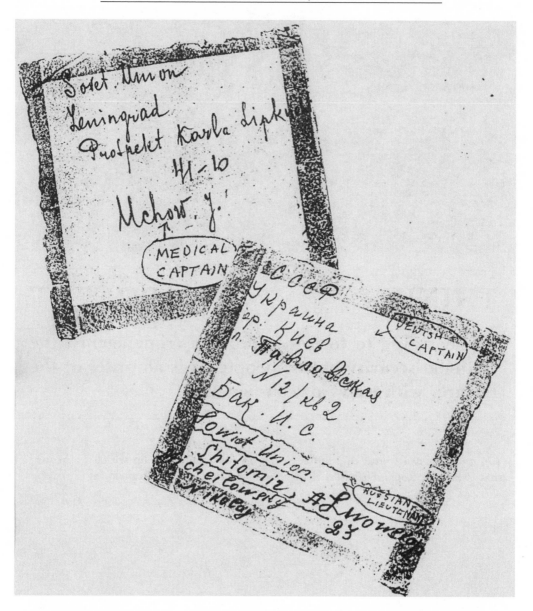

April 14, 1945 — After another 75 miles by truck we stopped in a village about eight miles from the Elbe River. Here I made the acquaintance of three Russian officers who had escaped from a P.O.W. camp. They made me the guest of honor at an impromptu celebration they held. They wrote their home addresses on the scraps of paper above. I planned to ask my folks to write to their folks to say they were alive and well.

That night, while on guard, I saw the searchlight in Berlin, about 60 miles away, go into action against an Allied air raid.

April 15, 1945 — GRIEBEN — My portrait is drawn by Emerson. On the left, he applies the finishing touches. On the right, a self-timed photo taken during the sketching. This is in exchange for the photos I took of him. He is a fine professional artist.

133

April 19, 1945 — GRIEBEN — A quiet afternoon on the front line! Kearns is chatting with a visitor. The Elbe River is just over the rise of ground along which our foxholes have been dug. The enemy is only a hundred yards away across the river. We arrived here on April 15.

I'm cooking a K ration in our foxhole.

*Opposite, bottom:* Kearns partakes of a package from home. The holes in his jacket are from shrapnel.

April 21–26, 1945 — BUCH on the Elbe river — Our last combat duty. Here we saw green flares the Russians fired to show they were in the vicinity. On the morning of the 27th, we climbed on trucks and were driven to Hamelin for occupation duty.

*Above:* May 1–8, 1945 — HAMELIN — This is a self-timed photo of me guarding the records of Nazi Storm Trooper Headquarters in the town of Hamelin of Pied Piper fame.

1st Squad, 1st Platoon, E Company, 137th Regiment, 35th Division. *Left to right, back:* Petrie, *, Joe Jacobsen, Vernon Kearns, *, Cooper. *Front:* Swenson, Cross, *, *, Leff. *Replacements whose names I can't recall after over half a century.

May 2, 1945 — The war is still not over as can be seen by the passwords written in pencil at the top of this copy of "Stars and Stripes." NIMBLE is the challenge word to be answered by the counter sign word NUMB.

Hitler's demise ended the shooting war for us!

138

May 3, 1945 — REHER — 7 km from Hamelin. Today I arrived at this chair factory that had been converted into a Displaced Persons Camp. Everyone here is a Russian slave laborer or liberated P.O.W. Because I could make myself understood in German, I was asked to help procure food for the camp. The Pass/Permit at the top of the next page was issued to me for that purpose.

*3 May '45*

*This driver has permission to drive this automobile for the purpose of procuring food for the D.P. camp at Keter, Germany, only.*

*Don P. Askell*
*1st Lt. Inf.*

*Void after 5 May, 1945.*

**TO ALL MEMBERS OF THE ALLIED EXPEDITIONARY FORCE:**

The task which we set ourselves is finished, and the time has come for me to relinquish Combined Command.

In the name of the United States and the British Commonwealth, from whom my authority is derived, I should like to convey to you the gratitude and admiration of our two nations for the manner in which you have responded to every demand that has been made upon you. At times, conditions have been hard and the tasks to be performed arduous. No praise is too high for the manner in which you have surmounted every obstacle.

I should like, also, to add my own personal word of thanks to each one of you for the part you have played, and the contribution you have made to our joint victory.

Now that you are about to pass to other spheres of activity, I say Good-bye to you and wish you Good Luck and God-Speed.

*Dwight Eisenhower*

This farewell message from General Eisenhower brought an end to the war.

# POSTSCRIPT

In November of 1996 I came into possession of a Company E Roster. I tried contacting every familiar name. Many of the letters I sent came back unopened. Many never came back at all. Of those who could, several people agreed to join me for a reunion in Topeka, Kansas.

After half a century, this meeting had a great emotional impact on all of us. We devoted one full day to visiting Holton, Kansas, less than an hour's drive north of Topeka. In Holton we spent some emotional moments around a monument to the Company E men killed in World War II.

To me two names had special meaning. Sgt. Rich was a jovial, very friendly guy with whom I shared a

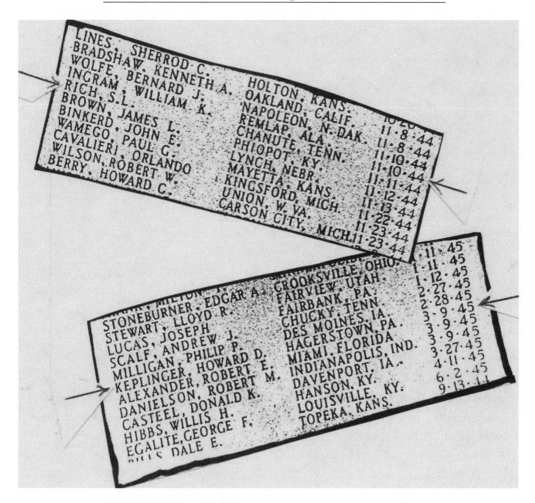

foxhole many times. He was killed during our attack on Malaucourt. Howard Keplinger helped me dig my first foxhole — a sincere, kindly soul. He was killed in Ossenberg.

Now, over fifty years later, I see their loss in a different light. We, the survivors, have had families, children and grandchildren they could never have. It is only necessary to review the names of each person in our own families to really understand the full impact of their sacrifice.

My emotional state before combat was built on a lifetime of healthy contact with reality. I could and did accept things as they were with a feeling of certainty that I never questioned.

Combat was different!

Things were happening that were so extreme, so unbelievable, my mind had trouble accepting them as real. At the time, I felt it must be what we referred to in childhood as "make-believe." The word "unbelievable" took on a literal meaning. I had a problem believing what I was experiencing. For me this was an insight into the mind of an insane person, where reality is open to question. With the return to the stability of civilian life, this feeling became a unique memory.

It was not until the war was over that I heard of all the horrors the Nazis inflicted on the people of the world and especially against the Jewish people. Being Jewish, I felt a peculiar satisfaction in knowing that I, at least, was able to shoot back.

With the perspective of over half a century and several wars since that time, America's behavior during World War II seems all the more remarkable. We were fighting a ruthless, determined, highly successful military machine of unprecedented power. They were unstoppable. But stop them we did, with much blood and tears. The country was never more united.

Banners with a star for each member of the family in the armed forces hung in windows everywhere. My parents had a banner with two stars. One star was for my brother and the other was for me. With both children in the Army they lived in constant fear and hope. However, they knew everyone else was also committed to victory. There really was no option.

On returning home, I had one of the greatest emotional moments of my life when I walked through the door of my parents' home. While in combat I had resigned myself to the fact that this could not, would not happen. In foxholes all over Europe I had considered this moment as an unlikely fantasy. My mother, father and grandmother almost crushed me in their embrace.

Later that night I got back into my old familiar bed but I could not fall asleep. A combination of elation, thankfulness and incredulity whirled around in my head.

In the days that followed, walking down familiar streets I came to realize how easy and comfortable it was to walk without all that heavy equipment to which I had grown accustomed. And best of all, no one was shooting at me! It was truly a high point in my life.

Years later, while getting ready for bed and adjusting the window blinds, I looked out at my snow-covered back yard and was reminded of the Battle of the Bulge. Even on a dark night the white snow helped you see. I was hunkered down at the bottom of my foxhole. It was cold, very cold. My feet stopped feeling cold. Now they hurt. How to keep warm? For me, shivering seemed to help. A raincoat over my head redirected my warm breath to the rest of my body. That also seemed to help. Incoming shells switched my attention from being miserable and unbearably cold to basic survival. But that didn't last. What I wouldn't give to be back home in my own warm bed. But that would come later.

Seven men from my platoon came to the meeting I organized in 1996 in

Topeka. I had thought of them through the years. What were they like now? Over half a century had passed. In my mind's eye these people had taken on a mythic quality. Through the intervening years the war itself had become an historic event. Two full generations had come into being. These, my war buddies, were becoming historic figures in my mind. In the motel, before I actually saw him I heard Ray Lux's voice. I felt like Jules Vernes's time machine had dropped me back in time.

That this was a highly emotional time for all of us there can be no doubt. Of course we recalled many hair-raising incidents we shared. We told jokes and socialized and before we knew it those fifty odd years simply evaporated. Most of us brought our wives. My wife had been somewhat anxious because she hadn't met many people from other parts of the country before. I was surprised at how quickly the wives became really good friends. Though their backgrounds were different they had much more in common than they expected.

Topeka was chosen because it was only an hour's drive to the town of Holton where Company E had a memorial to its war dead. Our pilgrimage there is one none of us will forget. Reading the names engraved on the monument made us realize that this was more than a social gathering. At one time each of the names was a person like ourselves. While we had lived full lives, they had not. When we parted we could not know what the future had in store for us. As I write this two of the eight are now gone.

Every year the 35th Infantry Division Association holds a reunion in a city chosen by its president. After the informal reunion of 1996 described above, I started attending the association's annual reunions. Here veterans from every unit that served with the 35th assemble to share three days of interesting and moving events. While my initial interest was with people I knew during the war, I now was making good friends from other regiments and service companies.

The association also publishes a newspaper to which I contribute frequently. In addition I am now a member of the Executive Board and Publicity Chairman for the association.

An important part of the reunion is our memorial service where we hear the names of members who have passed away since our last meeting. As our membership dwindles we are reinvigorated by the influx of the children of members invited to join the association as equal members. For me the most poignant of these are the children of 35th soldiers killed in action over half a century ago. Obviously the future of the 35th Division Association will depend on this new generation.

In July of 2004 the 35th Infantry Division Association sponsored a tour of our battlefields in France, Belgium, Luxembourg and Holland. In St. Lo, Normandy, a block-long honor guard of armed French soldiers, sailors and marines stood at attention in the rain. It was a celebration of the liberation of St. Lo by the 35th exactly 60 years before. We were their honored guests. In the city of Orleans, the 35th was celebrated as the savior of the city, as was Joan of Arc centuries before. In Lorraine, the city of Nancy gave us a sensational reception. Each of us was made the personal guest of an individual distinguished citizen at a lavish banquet in their very beautiful medieval City Hall.

When we reached Bastogne, I had an encounter with an ordinary citizen that touched me very much. The Battle of the Bulge which swirled around Bastogne was a very grim memory for me. This man who chanced by came up to me and said in English, "Thank You!" It was good to know what we did there was still appreciated by the average man.

As with the other cities, Luxembourg treated us royally with gifts and mementoes. The people of Venlo, Holland, went all out by driving us around the city in restored American G.I. trucks complete with 35th Division markings on the bumpers. As we passed by, whole families from grandfather to grandchild greeted us enthusiastically. The terrible years of Nazi terror were burned into the culture of these cities and their liberation became an important part of their history, part of their very ethos.

Of course we visited several American military cemeteries. Row after row of crosses and the occasional Star of David seemed to go on forever. One such cemetery was in Margraten, Holland. There, with the help of the internet, I found and

visited the grave of Howard Keplinger. We used to call him Kap. I had just arrived on the front line for the first time. This was my introduction to life and death on the front line; real death, not the movie version. There were only a few hours left to dig a foxhole before dark. Without being asked, Kap showed my partner and me how to dig this new version of a foxhole, and then he pitched right in helping us dig. Although this new environment had unnerved me, I can still remember how grateful I was for this unsolicited help. Kap was a kind and affable soul.

We made one stop in Ossenberg, Germany. As we passed by it, I recognized one of the buildings (shown on the previous page) as the same one pictured on page 83.

I got out of the bus and stood on the same spot almost sixty years before when I took that picture. The sun was shining. Flowers were blooming. Everything was as neat and orderly as could be. It was a unique, almost metaphysical experience. Kap Keplinger was killed and Ray Lux was wounded in that house. I was almost dizzy trying to sort out the present from the past, the real from the unreal. Lifting my camera and taking a picture of the house brought me back to the present. By now I realized the people in the bus were waiting for me. Off I went with still another indelible impression in my head.

# APPENDIX I

While I could not see more than two foxholes at any one time, the colonel in command of the 137th Regiment was getting the "Big Picture" from subordinates all over the front line. This information was recorded in daily reports that were marked "Secret" and sent up the chain of command. Eventually, many years later, these reports were declassified and made available in the National Archives. The very detailed official records which follow are known as After Action Reports.

Each report that concerns an event discussed earlier in this book was extracted and can be referenced to my account by simply matching the dates. Thus it is possible to compare my knowledge of a specific situation with that of the Regimental Commander. The following excerpts focus on my unit, Company E of the 2nd Battalion of the 137th Regiment of the 35th Division.

1. In compliance with the provisions of Par 10 C3 AR 345-105, submitted below is report after action against the enemy for the 137th Infantry covering the period 1–31 October 1944.

## 1 October 1944

On the morning of October 1 the 137th Infantry was opposed by strong German forces from a point midway between Pettoncourt and Chambrey on the Seille River northward to the edge of the Gremercey Forest.

DECLASSIFIED
Authority *NND 735067*
By _____ NARA Date *5/28/98*

HEADQUARTERS 137TH INFANTRY
APO 35          U S ARMY

S-E-C-R-E-T

Auth: CG 35th Inf Div
Initials _____
Date __*11 Nov 44*__

31 Oct 44                    DPD
                            590

The 137th Infantry strengthened its defenses during the day, using barbed wire between Chambrey and our positions to the north, and laying extensive mine fields on all possible routes of approach.

On October 2 one man was killed and four were wounded. Two enemy were taken prisoner, one of whom told of seeing the German V-3 one-man flying bomb which was to be used as a new weapon against the Allies.

After a week's defense of the area and after standing off the heaviest German attacks yet encountered by this organization, our main line of resistance had actually been pushed forward and strengthened. Lieutenant General Patton visited the Regimental CP and personally congratulated Colonel Sears on the fine stand of the organization, and decorated the Regimental Commander with the Bronze Star award during his visit.

## 2 October 1944

The 1st and 2nd Battalions were alerted for any possible enemy movement, but during most of the day October 2 there was no enemy action to our front.

## 3–4–5 October 1944

On October 3 the 137th Infantry improved its defensive position and conducted patrols, with very little enemy action reported.

The enemy continued to shell our area intermittently during October 3, 4 and 5, particularly in Pettoncourt and Gremercey, where 105 and 150 mm artillery was reported.

Rain which had been threatening for several days began to fall during the morning of the 5th, and continued through the day.

Casualties for October 3rd to 5th were as follows: three men wounded on the 3rd, 1 man wounded and two missing on the 4th, and four men killed and one wounded on the 5th.

Only two prisoners were taken on the 3rd, and none on the 4th or 5th.

## 6–7 October 1944

On October 6 and 7 the regiment remained in Division reserve. Scattered enemy artillery fire continued, and German planes were reported over the area in small numbers as the weather began to clear.

There were no casualties on the 6th, and on the 7th one man was killed, one wounded and one missing.

## October 1944

The remainder of the 137th continued in Division reserve at Attilloncourt and Gremercey during this time. Intermittent shelling was received in their area with little damage. Shell fragments recovered were over 2 inches wide by 1½ inches thick and up to 14 inches long, and indicated that the shells were from 280 mm railway guns.

## 12–13–14–15 October 1944

From October 12 to 15 the 2nd Battalion continued to report intermittent shelling in Gremercey, but damage was negligible. The only casualties in the regiment during this period occurred on October 13, when one man was killed and one wounded.

## 16 October 1944

From October until the end of the month the 137th Infantry remained in a defensive status. The right portion of the sector was occupied by the 2nd Battalion, and was bounded by the northern edge of the Jallaucourt Woods and the Gremercey Forest to a point south of Fresnes, where the lines of the 320th Infantry began.

With the assistance of the 60th Engineer Battalion, elaborate defense installations were established along our lines, with mine fields, booby traps, concertina fencing, and trip flares used extensively.

To the front of this line, our Engineers blew up the bridges across the Rau d'Osson on the road southwest of Malaucourt, on the Jallaucourt-Manhoue Road, and due south of Jallaucourt.

The 2nd Battalion's line was equally divided between Company G on the left and Company E on the right.

## 17 October 1944

Early on the morning of October 17 Company E fired on a German patrol which set off a trip-wire flare to their front. Mortar fire on the area was believed to have inflicted casualties on the Germans.

The 2nd Battalion received 120 mm mortar fire southeast of Jallaucourt at 1450. At 1840 they again reported shelling, with eighteen to twenty rounds believed to have been fired into their area from tanks.

During the evening the Germans began sending up flares, and this continued all night. Seventeen flares were observed during the night, mostly in the vicinity of Malaucourt, Jallaucourt and Aulnois. The regiment had only one casualty during the day, one man being wounded by enemy artillery fire.

## 18–19–20 October 1944

During the period of October 18, 19 and 20 the 137th Infantry was encountering very little enemy action.

On October 18 and 19 the 137th Infantry made preparations for possible isolation from the Division CP during the week to follow. Sixteen miles to the east of our area, near Dieuze, was the Etang de Lindre, a large artificial lake formed by the damming of the Seille River at Lindre Basse. By blowing out the earth dam there, the Seille River Valley could be flooded, circling our area.

For the 137th Infantry, October 20 was a day of increased German artillery activity, but little other enemy action was observed. Company E later reported receiving long range machine gun fire. One 2nd Battalion patrol returned at 0700, after observing Jallaucourt for 1½ hours.

The enemy's artillery activity began early on the morning of the 20th, and the 2nd Battalion received ten rounds of 88 fire at 0645. Two direct hits were scored on the Battalion CP, and communications were disrupted but no casualties resulted. Shortly before 1500 Company E received 88 fire.

The regiment had no casualties on October 18 or 19 but on October 20 one man was killed and two wounded by artillery fire, and three men were missing in action.

## 21 October 1944

Enemy artillery fire slackened during the day, and that which was received fell in front of our lines. At 1900 Company E again received long range machine gun fire from the Juree Woods, but no casualties resulted.

## 22–23 October 1944

The skies began to clear on the 22nd, after rain had fallen intermittently for most of the past week. The dirt roads in the sector had already been churned into a mass of deep mud, and water in foxholes and slit trenches added to the discomfort of the troops.

At 0415 an outpost of Company E reported a motorized column moving into Fresnes from the northwest. At the road junction west of Fresnes the column split up, half turning toward Jallaucourt and half continuing to Fresnes. The vehicles remained in town only a short time, then returned to the road junction west of Fresnes and turned northwest toward Lemoncourt. Our artillery shelled the road junction as the vehicles converged there.

During the day the 2nd Battalion spotted a battery of 88 mm self-propelled guns north of Fresnes, and called for an air strike on the position.

The Seille River flood reached its highest stage in our sector late on the 22nd. During the morning of October 23 the river began to fall at Pettoncourt, as the flood crest began to move north into German territory.

Both 2nd and 3rd Battalions received artillery fire during the morning of October 23. The 2nd Battalion received eleven rounds from 0630 to 0650, with seven rounds of 88s in the Company E area.

The regiment had had one man missing in action on the 23rd, their first loss since October 20.

## 22–23 October 1944

Few prisoners were taken by any of the units along the Corps front, and that mission became a high priority among our nightly patrols. One party attempted to enter enemy-held Malaucourt intent on seizing and bringing back a German soldier. The patrol reached the first house on the west edge of the town, when it was discovered and three enemy machine guns opened up on them. The patrol was forced to withdraw after two of its members had been wounded. Both the wounded men were evacuated safely to our lines.

The 2nd Battalion again sent patrols toward the Jallaucourt-Fresnes road, and reported that route to be strongly outposted by the enemy. Repeated attempts were made by one patrol to approach the road at several points, and each attempt drew small arms fire.

Company E reported concentrations of enemy artillery fire fell in their area shortly after 1000, and during the evening the same company began receiving direct fire from what was believed to be a self-propelled gun in the vicinity of Frenes.

## 27 October 1944

During the early morning of October 27 there was increased activity of horse-drawn wagons and carts in the Juree Woods, in Jallaucourt and Malaucourt, and on the road between.

## 30 October 1944

Aside from early patrol activity, October 31 was comparatively quiet, and there were no casualties in the regiment, and no enemy shellfire was reported.

Rpt after Action against Enemy
Hq 137th Inf 31 Oct 44

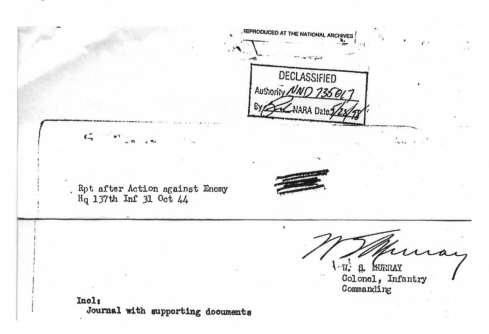

REPRODUCED AT THE NATIONAL ARCHIVES

DECLASSIFIED
Authority *NND 735017*
By ___ NARA Date ___

Rpt after Action against Enemy
Hq 137th Inf 31 Oct 44

W. B. MURRAY
Colonel, Infantry
Commanding

Incl:
Journal with supporting documents

HEADQUARTERS 137TH INFANTRY
APO 35      U S ARMY

Dec 44

Subject: Report after Action against Enemy

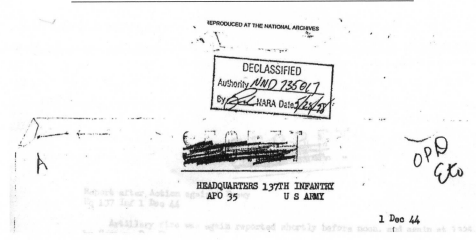

HEADQUARTERS 137TH INFANTRY
APO 35          U S ARMY

1 Dec 44

To The Adjutant General
Washington 25, D C.
Through: Command Channels

1. In compliance with the provisions of Par 10 03, AR 345-105, submitted below is report after action against the enemy for the 137th Infantry covering the period 1–30 November 1944

# 1 November 1944

November 1 found the 137th Infantry in its sixth week in a defensive status, as XII Corps continued its mission of defending that portion of the Third Army front from ten miles south of Metz, to twenty miles east of Nancy. The 35th Division was bounded on the left by the 80th Division, and on the right by the 26th.

Within our sector, the 2nd Battalion came out of reserve on November 1, with Companies E, F and G on the line from right to left.

# 3 November 1944

Showers fell intermittently during the day, and all was quiet to our front until after dark, when enemy patrols became active. At 2025 Company E reported a patrol to its front, but rifle fire forced the Germans to withdraw.

# 6 November 1944

One man of the regiment was wounded on November 6, and one enemy prisoner taken.

Rains swelled the Seille River to flood stage, and for the second time in two weeks the valley was inundated as far as Ajoncourt.

After its short period of inactivity, the Third Army prepared to resume the offensive. In the Metz-Nancy area, to encircle the German fortress city of Metz, and to continue the drive on the Siegfried line.

At 1330 on November 7, Division Field Order No. 26 was passed down to the officers of the 137th Infantry; after more than six weeks in a defensive status, they were again prepared to attack.

The initial mission of the 137th Infantry was to attack to the north and northeast, secure bridgehead across the Rau d'Osson and seize the first objective, five miles to the northeast of our present position.

# 8 November 1944

The regiment attacked at 0600 on the morning of November 8, after a heavy artillery preparation. The 2nd Battalion, on the left, encountered the first resistance, one enemy machine gun at 0611. On the right, the 1st Battalion attacked Jalloucourt, and by 0720 had one platoon of Company C in the town. Two platoons were pinned down west of the town by heavy enemy fire.

In the 2nd Battalion sector, two platoons of Company E reached the edge of Malaucourt by 0750, but to their left Company G was encountering difficulty in crossing the swollen Rau d'Osson, where flood waters of the Seille River had backed up into the stream. By 1000 all of Company G were across and on the ridge northwest of Malaucourt. At the same time, Company E was in the town, had cleaned out four buildings, and was working its way on through, house by house.

Steady rain set in shortly after noon, and our air support was called off during the afternoon.

By midafternoon the enemy had been cleared from all but the north edge of Jallaucourt, and at 1500 the 3rd Battalion was ordered to move companies to both Malaucourt and Jallaucourt to relieve troops there. (*I never saw them!*)

A second bridge was completed by the engineers at 1610, south of Malaucourt, and at 1630 Company F crossed on tanks and moved into town, where Company E was still engaged. Direct artillery fire was received and the lead tank was knocked out. The remaining tanks fanned out, and Company F dismounted and proceeded on foot. At 1750 both Company F and Company E were on the north edge of town, and at this time orders were received from the Division Commander to hold up the attack at 1800, consolidate positions and outpost security, and to prepare to attack the following morning at 0600.

On this the first day of the new offensive, the 137th Infantry took 134 prisoners, most of them from the 1125th Regiment. Our casualties on the same day were 6 killed and 76 wounded. Lieutenant Victor W. Schultz of Company C was killed in the attack on Jallaucourt.

# 9 November 1944

The regiment resumed the attack at 0600 on the 9th, with the 1st Battalion striking toward Oriocourt, two miles northeast of Jallaucourt. The 2nd Battalion, leaving Company I to clean out the last resistance in Malaucourt, moved north, and at 0755 Company G called for lifting of our artillery fire on the Aulnois Woods and attacked the German positions there. Company E and Company F followed closely. Moderate resistance was encountered 150 yards inside the woods, but the battalion advanced steadily during the morning, and at 1400 had cleared the woods. The Battalion then reorganized and moved toward Lemoncourt.

At 1415 the 2nd Battalion captured Lemoncourt, taking 50 prisoners. At 1915 the 2nd Battalion captured Delme, two kilometers north. The Germans withdrew to the east, and began shelling the town heavily with mortar and artillery fire.

# 10 November 1944

The 2nd Battalion set out to capture Viviers, and to occupy the woods south of the town. The Battalion, operating with armor, attacked Viviers from the south shortly before 1100. Here they met stiff resistance from the Germans who had moved into the town during the night. In addition to small arms fire from the town, the Battalion began receiving long range artillery fire from the east. At 1245 they had not yet been able to enter the town, and our tanks were having difficulty in maneuvering off the roads due to the mud.

The 2nd Battalion, after fighting most of the afternoon, had Company F and one platoon from Company E in Viviers by 1600. An hour later, two full companies were in the town, and fighting was still going on. At 1800 Viviers was aflame, and the 2nd Battalion occupied most of the town. Fifty Germans had been taken prisoner and many more wounded or killed.

# 12 November 1944

The attack was resumed at 0800 on November 11, and the 2nd Battalion quickly cleared Viviers of the Germans left there and at 0830 moved northeast toward the Serres Woods.

The 2nd Battalion began to clear the way toward Oron through the Serres Woods. With tanks in support they moved from Viviers to the edge of the woods, and by noon two companies, E and G, were in the woods.

In the Serres Woods, Company E and Company G advanced steadily until 1600, when they were held up by two pill boxes and two tanks protecting the road junction halfway through the woods. Tank destroyers were brought up, and at 1815 this resistance was knocked out, and the two companies pushed on to the road junction.

# 13 November 1944

On November 13 enemy resistance stiffened, as the 137th Infantry hit a strong defense line from the woods north of Villers-sur-Neid to Achain. Jumping off at 0800, the 3rd Battalion attacked northeastward, while to the north the 2nd Battalion advanced on Villers-sur-Neid. Both received heavy artillery and mortar fire immediately after jumping off. After two hours' fighting, Company G pushed on into Villers, and at 1130 two companies were in the town. Street fighting was in progress until shortly after noon, when our forces cleared the town of Germans. The 2nd Battalion then reorganized and continued the attack toward Marthille, a mile to the east, which they entered at 1530 and captured at 1700 after a fight. After taking Marthille, the battalion quickly moved on Destry, two miles northeast.

The 2nd Battalion, in their attempt to capture Destry, reached the ridge south of the town at 1700, where they were stopped by heavy mortar and artillery fire. With the 4th Armored Division moving into the area, an attack on Destry the following morning with that unit was decided upon.

The 1st Battalion, still in reserve, moved to Marthille at 1600. This day was the coldest yet, and during the night snow fell over the entire sector.

# 14 November 1944

The 2nd and 3rd Battalions resumed the attack at 0900 on the 14th. The 2nd Battalion attacked Destry with the 4th Armored. However, the armor was held up one kilometer south of the town until almost noon by enemy artillery. Shortly after noon the tanks entered the town, and Companies E and G fought their way in at the same time. Here again house-to-house fighting resulted, and the town was not fully occupied by our troops until late afternoon. Securing the town, the 2nd Battalion held up for the night but sent patrols to the front as far as the railroad two kilometers northeast, which was the Division objective.

Casualties in the regiment were 2 killed and 29 wounded on the 14th. There were 34 prisoners taken. Prisoners captured during the past two days gave the information that they were recently brought from the Polish front and placed in Marthille, Baronville and other points in the sector; that they had been given no orientation on the situation, only told to hold these towns at all cost.

# 15 November 1944

On November 15 the 137th Infantry, nearing the Division objective, continued the attack for the eighth consecutive day. Both 2nd and 3rd Battalions moved to seize the Metz-Benestroff railway in their zone.

Jumping off at 0900, the 2nd Battalion was the first to reach the railroad, and moved on to the objective at 1035.

# 16 November 1944

On November 16, after eight days of continuous fighting, the 137th Infantry gained a brief rest, remaining in their present position and awaiting further orders.

The enemy had left the area heavily mined, and although these were being cleared as quickly as possible, some casualties resulted from this menace on the 16th. The regiment also continued to receive scattered artillery shelling. Casualties on the 16th were one killed, seven wounded and four missing. Twelve Germans were taken prisoner.

# 17 November 1944

The regiment continued to remain in their present position on November 17. There was no let up in the cold weather, and the skies were overcast. A light snow fell late in the day.

The order to continue the attack was received, and at 1330, Regimental Field Order No. 22 was issued, calling for the 1st and 3rd Battalions to attack at 0800 the following morning. The ultimate objective was the Saar River at a point south of Sarrguemines.

The 2nd Battalion, after having been on the line all the way from Malaucourt to la Houve, was placed in regimental reserve for the coming operation.

# 18–19 November 1944

On the 19th the 2nd Battalion moved up to Gros Tenquin during the night to relieve the 1st Battalion.

# 20 November 1944

The 2nd Battalion jumped off at 0900, in conjunction with the 6th Armored, and moved to attack the Freybouse Woods to their front. Heavy artillery fire was received as the battalion jumped off and advanced steadily and at 1015 punched into the woods north of the Gros-tenquin-Hellimer highway. By noon they cleared the woods in their zone. Emerging from the east end of the woods, however, the battalion was subjected to terrific fire from the high ground to the north and east. With perfect observation, the Germans brought deadly mortar, small arms and direct artillery fire on our troops with every attempt to advance over the open terrain to the front. By darkness the battalion had made no appreciable gain, and the attack was stopped for the night.

Six officers were wounded in the day's attack, the largest loss in a single day among officers since the Moselle River crossing.

Casualties among enlisted men were 4 killed, 51 wounded and 6 missing. Forty-two Germans were captured on the 20th.

## 21 November 1944

The 2nd Battalion resumed its attack toward Hellimer on the 21st. Again attempting to advance east along the Hellimer highway, they moved 500 yards past the Francaltroff road junction, when enemy small arms fire opened up. From 1730 until almost 0900 they again were subjected to heavy fire from their front. Tanks of the 6th Armored moved up at 0900, and together they advanced toward Hellimer. Shortly after noon they were in a position to attack the town, but the first assault was thrown back by heavy machine gun and tank fire. The battalion attacked again at 1300, but the Germans had five tanks in the northwest corner of the town holding up the approach, and it was almost 1500 before any sizable force could get into the town. The Germans were cleared from the town house to house. Two enemy tanks were knocked out in the fight, and another abandoned in perfect condition as the Germans withdrew to Diffembach to the northeast.

Three of our men were killed on the 21st, and fifty-five were wounded. Thirty-eight Germans were captured.

## 22 November 1944

On the morning of the 22nd, forces of the 3rd Battalion cleared Fremestroff early, and the 2nd Battalion moved on to Diffembach, where the Germans had gone from Hellimer. Company E was first in the town, and pushed the enemy out shortly after noon. The rest of the battalion moved up, and at 1400 jumped off for Hilsprich, four kilometers east.

The 2nd Battalion moved half the distance to Hilsprich, then was counterattacked at 1540 by Germans from the Habsat Woods north of the Hellimer-St Jean highway. The enemy was stopped with severe losses from our combined machine gun and mortar fire, and the surviving Germans fled back into the woods.

Six men were killed, seventeen wounded and five missing in action in the regiment on November 22. There were fifty eight prisoners captured, including members of the 36th SS Division.

# 23 November 1944

On the morning of November 23 all battalions were attacking. The 2nd jumping off at 0800 from the high ground midway between Diffembach and Hilsprich, moved through the Machweld Woods and swung right, to the southeast of Hilsprich.

The 2nd Battalion entered the woods north of Zellen at 0930, and by noon was emerging from the southeast tip of the woods. Here they received direct fire from the high ground to the east, and were pinned down and unable to advance during the afternoon.

Total casualties in the regiment were ten killed, seventy six wounded and forty missing. Sixteen Germans were captured on the 23rd.

# 24 November 1944

The 2nd Battalion held their position southwest of Hilsprich, covering any possible enemy withdrawal to the south. The battalion then outposted the high ground to the southwest with one platoon of Company F, and the remainder of the battalion moved back to Diffembach.

# 25–26–27 November 1944

On the 25th the 2nd Battalion moved to the Hilsprich area to occupy the town and prevent reoccupation by the Germans.

On the 26th and 27th the 137th Infantry remained in place and continued patrolling and strengthening defenses in its area. The skies cleared on the 26th, for the first time in over a week.

# 28–29–30 November 1944

On November 28 the 137th Infantry moved to an area approximately seven miles to the west with the 2nd Battalion at Bistroff.

On the 29th and 30th the regiment remained in its areas to gain a well-earned rest. There were no casualties during the last three days of the month. Two Germans were taken prisoner on the 29th.

The month of November had developed some of the hardest fighting yet engaged in by the 137th Infantry. Although comparatively inactive the first week, the regiment was in the attack more days during November than any previous month. Since November 8 our troops had advanced over thirty miles to the northeast against the most stubborn resistance. They had captured thirty-three towns, and taken nearly 1500 prisoners.

Our own casualties in the drive had not been light. We had lost 76 killed, 573 wounded and 98 missing. However, of those missing, only 66 were unaccounted for at the end of the month.

In this drive, the 137th Infantry had played an important part in the great Third Army offensive which already had resulted in the capture of Metz and the crossing of the Saar River.

Forward elements of our own regiment now stood eleven miles from the German border at Sarreguemines, twenty-two miles southwest of the industrial city of Saarbrucken, and awaited the orders which would carry them into the Reich itself.

Report after Action against Enemy
Hq 137 Inf 1 Dec 44

W. S. MURRAY
Colonel, Infantry
Commanding

1 Incl
Unit Journals w/supporting papers.

HEADQUARTERS 137TH INFANTRY
APO 35                    US ARMY

1 January 1945

Report After Action against Enemy
Hq '137 Inf 1 Dec 44

W. S. MURRAY
Colonel, Infantry
Commanding

1 Incl
Unit Journals w/supporting papers,

HEADQUARTERS 137TH INFANTRY
APO 35      US ARMY

1 January 1945

SUBJECT : Report After Action Against Enemy

TO      : The Adjutant General
           Washington 25, D.C.

1. In compliance with the provisions of Par 10 C3, AR 345105, submitted below is report after action against the enemy for the 137th Infantry covering the period 1–31 December 1944.

# December 1, 1944

This day marked the regiment's 146th day on French soil, 111 days of which were spent in actual combat, with 137th elements opposing the enemy on the front lines.

A training program was scheduled for this period of relative inactivity which consisted of pill-box assault activity, handling of demolitions, and staging of attacks on fortified positions.

# December 2, 1945

The 137th Infantry remained in reserve on the 2nd and made preparations to move the following day to a new assembly area.

# December 3, 1945

The 137th Infantry moved seven miles, approximately northeast, to its new assembly area on the morning of December 3 and remained in division reserve. Regimental Headquarters, Special Units and the 2nd Battalion closed into Erstroff by 1000.

# December 4, 1944

On this day the 137th Infantry remained in its assembly area and its status of Corps reserve.

# December 5, 1944

Again the 137th Infantry remained in its assembly areas as Corps reserve.

# December 6, 1944

The 137th Infantry made a motor movement, approximately fifteen miles east through the early morning rain of December 6 and closed into its forward assembly area by 0900.

# December 7, 1944

There was no change in the status of the 137th Infantry on this day.

# December 8, 1944

The 137th Infantry Regiment moved by foot to another forward assembly area approximately nine miles east in the direction of Sarreguemines, on December 8. The 2nd Bn moved into the Foret de Sarreguemines just past Siltheim.

All was quiet in the towns occupied by the 137th Infantry Regiment.

# December 9, 1944

The 137th Infantry was to attack the following morning, marching from its assembly area and across the Saar beginning at 0500 by using the railroad bridge south of the town. The 2nd and 3rd Battalions abreast, were to attack at 0730. The 2nd Battalion on the left was to take that portion of Saareguemines that lay north of the river and attempt to seize intact, the bridge that crossed the Blies River within its sector.

# December 10, 1944

The attack moved smoothly this day with the 3rd Battalion crossing the railroad bridge on the southeastern outskirts of Sarreguemines without receiving any enemy fire. The battalions completed the crossing by 0545. The 2nd Battalion completed crossing the river and closed into its assembly area north of the river. With poor visibility from an overcast sky, but no rain, the battalion jumped off at 0730.

The 2nd Battalion met bitter resistance from the enemy who was strongly organized. Company E cleaned out the buildings north of Sarreguemines. Co. E had tough opposition in these houses but finished routing out the enemy from their area.

# December 11, 1944

The 137th Infantry continued the attack on December 11 as the 2nd Bn cleaned out the remainder of Sarreguemines, liberating 995 Ex-PWs left behind by the Nazis.

At 0800, the 2nd and 3rd Battalions shoved off again as the 1st Battalion received orders to secure Sarreguemines on the eastern bank of the river after the 2nd Battalion moved on. The 1st Battalion was to follow the 2nd at 800 yards.

The 2nd Battalion experienced considerable difficulty in ridding Sarreguemines of the remaining enemy. All the buildings were honeycombed with passages and mouse-holed for machine gunners and snipers.

# December 12, 1944

At 0100, December 12, the 137th Infantry had the first man in the division to enter Germany. No crossings were to be attempted except with division approval.

The forward elements of the regiment were heavily shelled throughout the day and quite a few casualties were suffered. Frauenberg was rapidly turning into the hottest town ever occupied by 137th troops.

# December 13, 1944

While elements of the 137th Infantry's 3rd Bn crossed the Blies River into Germany at dawn on the morning of December 13 and encountered severe artillery fire throughout the day, the 2nd Battalion maintained contact between the 1st and 3rd.

# December 14, 1944

The 3rd Bn of the 137th Infantry was entirely across the Blies River into Germany shortly after midnight and on December 14 pushed ahead to the high ground north and northeast of the river. The 2nd Bn remained this side of the river and prepared to follow the 3rd Bn. Co E also was in a position protecting the left flank.

# December 15, 1944

Co E remained south of the Blies River and assisted the 1st Bn. The 2nd Bn was to be committed the following morning with the mission of capturing Bliesmengen and Bliesbalchen. Today's casualties were the heaviest of any day since the regiment started the Saar River operation.

## December 16, 1944

Pushed back to the edge of the Breitwald Woods by the enemy on December 15, the 3rd Bn of the 137th Infantry attacked again, the well defended enemy positions in the forest and regained a portion of the lost ground. The enemy artillery fire remained extremely heavy throughout the day and Frauenberg received its usual pounding of intense artillery and mortar fire. At the same time our air support bombed and staffed Bleismengen and the woods to the east of it. The 2nd Bn had G Co across the Blies protecting the rear flank of the 3rd Bn, while Co E was aiding the 1st Bn.

## December 17, 1944

137th Infantry elements were fighting under the heaviest artillery fire they had ever experienced in France or Germany.

The 3rd Bn forces in the Breiterwald Woods were unable to move against the savage enemy resistance and were taking a severe shelling all day. Our direct support artillery pounded enemy positions in the woods and the air support bombed and strafed the enemy positions unmercifully but the enemy still held tenaciously to the forest.

Elements of the 2nd Bn fighting in Bliesmengen were faced by direct enemy tank fire and other elements were pinned down all day. The enemy continued to shell the regimental area heavily during the period. Frauenberg was hit very heavily again and again during the day. All units of the 137th Infantry were alerted at 1125 for bomber support and at noon fighter bombers were hitting the enemy in the Bucholtz woods ahead of the regiment's positions. The 137th was ordered to resume the attack on December 18.

## December 18, 1944

The enemy was heavily pounded by P-47s in the regimental sector throughout the day. Breiterwald Woods was again the scene of fierce battles between German and American infantry and tanks. The enemy was unable to stop the assault of our forces and was driven back to the rear edge of the woods.

The regiment was ordered to stop its attack at 1830 and to consolidate its positions on most favorable ground. The 2nd Battalion had elements in Bliesmengen and east of the town.

## December 19, 1944

Frauenberg continued to receive terrific artillery and mortar fire. The enemy fired again and again at the Frauenberg-Habkirchen bridge but never scored a hit.

The 2nd Battalion also improved its positions and placed road blocks and mine fields on its flanks. Fire was directed on the enemy who was extremely active to the Bn front. The Bn command post was shelled heavily but no casualties resulted.

## December 20, 1944

The 2nd Bn remained in position on the high ground near the woods and improved their positions during the day. Cos F, E and G in that order were on the line. The Bn received heavy enemy artillery fire during the period. During one two and a half hour period 1,000 rounds of artillery and mortar fire fell on the ridge and portions of the woods held by the Bn.

## December 21, 1944

On December 21, the 137th Infantry received orders that it would be relieved by the 324th Infantry of the 44th Inf Di prior to 2400 that day. The regiment was to assemble temporarily in the vicinity of Frauenberg, Habkirchen and Neunkirch until ordered to move to an assembly area.

The 2nd Bn improved its positions and also delivered harassing fire on all known and observed targets.

The 2nd Bn was relieved by elements of the 324th Inf by 2200 and the units assembled to move to the new area.

## December 22, 1944

The 2nd Bn arrived at Remering from Neunkirch and was billeted by 0315 in the new assembly area. During the day an ordnance check was made of all ordnance items and several 50 calibers were tested for anti-aircraft defense.

The regiment received more replacements which helped raise the strength of units. The regiment received eight officers and 220 enlisted men.

The 35th Inf Div was ordered to move by combat team to Metz sometime during the day. Later the IP time was set at 2330. The 137th Infantry Combat Team less the 219th FA BN, cleared the IP at Puttelange by 2330 and moved northwest toward Metz and its new assembly area.

## December 23, 1944

The 137th CT motorized left Puttelange at 2330 on December 22 and moving through St Avold, Boulet, and Metz arrived at its destination, Moulins, by 0400. Moulins is just west of Metz.

The regiment rested and cleaned and repaired equipment. They also attended movies, washed clothes, uniforms, and etc.

# December 24, 1944

The 137th Infantry Regiment remained assembled in the German barracks in Moulins. At 1140 on December 24, the 35th Infantry Division was assigned to the XX Corps from the XII Corps.

# December 25, 1944

The day was spent in rest with small classes held for some of the replacements. 155 more replacements were also received which brought the 137th strength to T/O.

# December 26, 1944

On December 26, the 137th CT with the 127 FA Bn attached moved by motor from Metz at 0645 and closed into the assembly area in the vicinity of Nothomb, Belgium by 1450. Upon its arrival, the regiment moved forward and relieved elements of the 6th Cavalry in its zone.

The regimental motor column entered Belgium via Messancy, turned west and passed by the town of Arlon, passed through Pontellange and on to Nothomb. Regimental Headquarters was established in Nothomb, while the battalions moved on into Luxembourg. The 2nd Bn billeted itself in Holtz.

Upon arrival the Combat Team ceased and the 127th FA and the 219th FA reverted to Division Artillery control. During the night forward elements of the regiment moved forward and relieved elements of the 6th Cavalry which were screening in the 137th zone to the north. The 4th Armored Division was on the left of the 35th Division and the 26th Division was on the right flank of the division. The 137th was to attack on the morning of December 27, passing through the 6th Cavalry and with the 4th Armored Division relieve the pressure on the 101st Airborne Division which was surrounded in Bastogne.

# December 27, 1944

The 137th Infantry jumped off at 0800 on December 27 with the 2nd Bn on the right and the 3rd on the left. The 2nd crossed the Surre River at 1015 and by 1110 the first elements of Co G entered the town of Surre. Co E was held up by enemy machine gun fire and was unable to enter the town.

The regiment was ordered to halt its advance at 1730 and organize defensive positions no later than 2000. The 137th was to resume the attack at 0600 on December 28. Co E pushed out into the woods at 2100 and ran into strong enemy dug in positions. The enemy force to the front was identified as the 5th German Paratroop Division.

# December 28, 1944

The 1137th Infantry attacked north of Surre against all types of heavy enemy fire and drove eastward to assault Villers-la-Bonne-Eau.

The 2nd Bn with companies E, F, and G in that order were on the edge of the Surre Woods. The 2nd Bn driving into the woods, was in the direct face of direct tank fire and considerable mortar. Enemy tracked vehicles were located 600 yards to the direct front of Cos E and F.

The regiment was ordered to suspend the attack at 1800 and consolidate for the night and attack at 0800 the following morning. The Corps Commanding General warned all units to beware of enemy counter attacks during the night or early morning. The Surre Woods still contained many enemy troops.

# December 28, 1944

The 137th Infantry attacked again in the Surre Woods against bitter machine gun and tank fire. The regiment attacked to the northeast in its zone.

The 2nd Bn attacked through the woods following an air strike and met heavy tank and self-propelled fire. The Bn advanced against this fire to the last tip of the Surre Woods. The 2nd Bn had Companies E and G forward with Co E in Surre.

The 137th was ordered to cease its attack at 1800 and continue the attack on December 30 at 0800. All roads leading into the area were to be mined and blocked. Road blocks were to be in depth, several on each road. The regiment halted its attack and buttoned up for the night. Enemy artillery fire was very heavy in the regimental area during the night with the Regimental CP area receiving several barrages of rockets.

# December 30, 1944

The 137th patrolled vigorously to the front during the night while the front lines and rear areas received heavy artillery and rocket fire. The snow that had fallen the previous day had frozen over and the ground and roads were slick and slippery. Harlange and Villes-la-Bonne-Eau remained the main points of enemy resistance. The 2nd Bn had two companies on the edge of the Surre Woods, meeting heavy enemy fire from the vicinity of Harlange and Betlange.

At 0645 Co E advanced toward Harlange passing through Co G. The company advanced with moderate resistance until it reached within 400 yards of Harlange when it received severe machine gun and mortar fire which pinned it down. The enemy also opened up on the company delivering flanking fire from the right and left flank. The threat to the right flank was stopped. Co E withdrew from the open field under a protective barrage and moved up a draw on the left flank of the enemy to outflank the enemy position and ran into tough opposition near Betlange.

At 0645 the 3rd Bn held four buildings in Villers-la-Bonne-Eau and by 0900 the enemy activity and resistance in the town increased considerably. Enemy assault guns and SS troops moved into the town in the morning to reinforce the enemy garrison and armored guns moved in and around the town shooting into the houses occupied by elements of the 3rrd Bn. Two of these guns were knocked out by bazooka fire and the rest withdrew out of bazooka range and shelled the houses with direct fire. Heavy fighting continued all day in the town until Cos K and L were considered cut off from the rest of the battalion.

At 0520 Co I was counterattacked by the enemy who had positions in the woods to their front and at 0615, the 3rd Bn lost communications with the company. Contact was regained that same morning.

The 1st Bn jumped off at 1330 for the town of Villers-la-Bonne-Eau. Cos B and C entered the town at 1420 and occupied some of the buildings. Two enemy tanks rolled up to their positions and started shelling with direct fire. Men from the companies fired bazookas at them but the tanks kept just out of bazooka range and although several hit the tanks they did not knock them out. The elements of the two companies were forced to withdraw back to the cover of the woods.

At 1700 the regiment was ordered to dig in for the night and continue operations the following morning.

The 2nd Bn, less Co G, pulled back to the town of Surre and moved to north of Livarchamps. Co E took over the road blocks occupied by Co A.

Two hundred thirty-five men were reported missing from Co K and L. The majority of these men were believed to be captured in the town of Villers-la-Bonne-Eau, where they had been cut off for two days by enemy tanks and infantry.

Total casualties during the month were 31 killed in action, 286 wounded in action, 274 missing in action. Enemy prisoners captured during the month were 308.

W.S. MURRAY
Colonel, Infantry
Commanding

Report after Action ____ 'nst Enemy
Hq 137th Inf 1 Jan 4.

Total casualties during the month were: 31 killed in action, 286 wounded in action, 274 missing in action. Enemy prisoners captured during the month were 308.

W. S. MURRAY
Colonel, Infantry
Commanding

2 Incls:
1. Awards and Presentations
2. Unit Journal 2/supporting papers

HEADQUARTERS 137TH INFANTRY
APO 35          U S ARMY

1 February 1945

## HEADQUARTERS 137th INFANTRY
### APO 35          U S ARMY

1 February 1945

SUBJECT: Report After Action Against Enemy
TO       : Adjutant General
             Washington 25, D.C.

In compliance with provisions of Par 10 03, AR 345-105, submitted below is Report After Action Against Enemy for the 137th Infantry covering the period 1–31 January 1945.

## 1 January 1945

On the regiment's front today, the 137th Infantry was facing the toughest opposition it had yet met in its combat experience. Elements of K and L Companies were still cut off in Villers-la-Bonne-Eau. The 2nd Bn had Companies E and F west and southwest of the Belgian town and Co G on the regiment's right flank, in Luxembourg. German prisoners had stated that the SS Adolf Hitler Division and the 339th Nazi Infantry Regiment were on the 137th's front.

The 137th jumped off at 1330 on an attack toward Villers, after patrols had been sent ahead into the town. The attacking elements had difficulty with enemy infiltration parties working around the flanks. A large number of enemy faced Companies E and F and a bitter fight ensued. At 1700 Co E relieved Co I, which had been in the woods west of Villers. The regiment was ordered to halt its advance at 1810, dig in, mine the roads, and patrol to the front in preparation to stepping off again at 0800, January 2. In Villers, Companies K and L were slowly being cut to pieces by tank fire and flame throwers.

## 2 January 1945

The 137th Infantry continued to attack the defenses about the town of Villers-la-Bonne–Eau on January 2. Co E pressing from the south cleared enemy points. The enemy opposition continued to be strong, as units of the 137th were under enemy artillery, tank, mortar and machine gun fire throughout the day. The weather was bitter and cold.

Fighter bombers bombed and strafed Villers and then struck close to the 137th front line positions. Bitter fighting was carried on along the front.

The Division ordered operations to halt at 1755, the forward elements of the 137th dug in and sent patrols to the front during the night.

## 3 January 1945

On January 3 the 137th Infantry attacked again but was unsuccessful in taking the road junction west of Villers-la Bonne-Eau. Enemy tanks thwarted the maneuverings of the 1st and 2nd Bns. Heavy fire of all types was received by the regiment throughout the day. The 2nd Bn had Cos E and F attacking west of Villers-la-Bonne-Eau.

At 0900 the 1st Bn reported the enemy was infiltrating up the road from Villers toward the road junction, and artillery checked this move. 2nd Bn patrols reached the junction at noon, but were unable to take it. Both the 2nd and 3rd Bns faced heavy artillery. The advance was stopped at 1700, all units posted security and used patrols to keep contact with the enemy. Mines were also laid by the regiment.

The second group of men from the 137th left today for furloughs to the United States. The quota was one officer and 13 Enlisted Men from the regiment.

# 4 January 1945

Today the 137th hurled an attack at the road junction west of Villers, captured and defended the position against heavy enemy counterattacks. The intense enemy artillery fire forced heavy casualties on the regiment.

# 5 January 1945

The 137th Infantry struggled on January 5 against the stubborn resistance as the 1st Bn moved to a position behind the 2nd Bn and prepared to follow the 2nd Bn in an attack. The 2nd Bn supported the 1st by fire and awaited its arrival in their rear before moving out. The 2nd Bn cleared out infiltration parties and also mopped up the draw to its front.

Heavy fire was received by the regiment throughout the day. Three terrific barrages landed at 0720. Companies A and E turned back two enemy patrols. The regimental listening posts picked up several enemy armored vehicles moving in Villers during the night.

# 6 January 1945

The weather grew colder on January 6 and the 137th Infantry continued its pressure for the second day on Villers, after capturing the all important road junction. Heavy fire was received all along the regiment's front.

The organic and attached field artillery Bns continued to support the division attack firing TOTs on all towns and roads in the division sector. A heavy schedule of harassing fire continued throughout the day.

# 7 January 1945

Today marked the 11th day that the 137th Infantry had been struggling on against the well-defended town of Villers. The regiment continued to put pressure on the village as it was being ripped apart by thundering artillery. The 137th front was cut down to approximately half its previous width as the 6th Cavalry Grp took over the right portion of the regiment's sector. The 2nd Bn with E and F was on the right.

# 8 January 1945

Active patrolling was conducted against the enemy and harassing fire was delivered throughout the day as the 137th Infantry maintained its pressure on the enemy in the vicinity of Villers-la-Bonne-Eau.

The 2nd Bn continued to occupy its original positions on the right flank of the regiment with E and F on line.

The entire III Corps was to launch an attack into the Belgian Bulge on the morning of January 9. The 6th Armored Division was to attack on the left flank of the 35th Division.

## 9 January 1945

With the 1st Bn working on the left flank and the 2nd Bn on the right, the 137th Infantry launched an attack on January 9 to take Villers and the ground to its north, but the enemy checked the thrust. The regiment's zone was laid out so that the 137th would be pinched out by adjacent units.

The 2nd Bn hit toward Villers and also protected the right flank of the regiment's zone. E and G companies were on the line while Co F was in reserve.

The 137th Infantry suffered heavy casualties as the enemy stopped the attack.

The 2nd Bn was heavily shelled at 2335 by artillery and mortar fire.

## 10 January 1945

Supported by tanks and tank destroyers, the 137th Infantry pushed ahead against the enemy again on January 10, making a slight gain in capturing the much sought and fought for town of Villers-la-Bonne-Eau, a target of the regiment for the past thirteen days. The regiment attacked at 0915 with attached units of tanks and tank destroyers.

The 1st Bn with attached units advanced up the center of the 137th's sector and gained slightly.

With a company of tanks and tank destroyers attached to the 2nd Bn it entered Villers and by 1400 had two buildings on the edge of the battered town. Later in the afternoon, the entire village was cleared.

At 1400 the road leading from Lutremange was choked with enemy vehicles and an air strike and artillery pounded the column.

The 137th was to attack again at 0800, January 11, supported by tanks and tank destroyers. The regiment suffered heavy casualties today, the majority being from the 2nd Bn.

The 137th Infantry had one of its coldest days on January 11 as it took the town of Lutremange and was pinched out in its sector by 1700.

The 2nd Bn had patrols step off from Villers and advance toward Lutremange to determine whether the town was occupied by the enemy. By 1300 Companies E, F and G had patrols going through the town and found it to be clear. The Bn was supported by fire from our tanks and tank destroyers. Lutremange was found to be almost as badly demolished as Villers.

By 1700, the 137th Infantry was pinched out by the advance of the 134th and Task Force Fickett. The 137th then went into 35th Division reserve. The 2nd Bn remained in Lutremange.

# 12 January 1945

The 137th Infantry remained in 35th Division reserve on January 12, with the 2nd Bn in Lutremange.

# 13 January 1945

The 137th Infantry remained in Division reserve on January 13, with all units occupying their original towns. The regiment received its tentative defense plan which it was to follow if ordered by Division.

# 14 January 1945

The regiment remained in division reserve on January 14 and also conducted reconnaissance parties over the area which the regiment was to defend if ordered. Caution was exercised since the MLR of the tentative defense plan was in the vicinity of the present front lines.

# 15 January 1945

On January 15 the 137th Infantry remained in 35th Division reserve.

# 16 January 1945

The 137th Infantry conducted rehabilitation and training again on January 16 as the regiment remained in 35th Division reserve. 2nd Bn was located in Lutremange. The 35th Division was in III Corps control.

# 17 January 1945

On January 17 the regiment received orders that CT 137 would move by motor on January 18 to the Fort Mosselle Barracks in Metz, France. The combat team was to cease upon its arrival in Metz. Three Quartermaster Truck Companies would provide 89 trucks for transportation on the move down into France.

# 18 January 1945

CT 137 moved out of Belgium on the morning of January 18, exercising certain counter-intelligence measures and moved by motor to Metz, France.

Strict secrecy was observed on this move from Belgium to France, which included the covering of division patches, bumpers and any other markings which would disclose the unit. Route markers on this move did not show any unit designation or number. Fort Moselle is located in northern Metz.

# 19 January 1945

The 137th Infantry was billeted in Fort Moselle Barracks, within walking distance of downtown Metz.

At 1620, CT 137 was placed in XX Corps reserve as per Corps Operatons Instructions No. 50, 19 January 45, and was ordered to be prepared to move by motor on a three hour notice.

# 20–21–22 January 1945

From January 20 to 22, the 137th Infantry remained in Corps reserve and was on a three hour notice to leave Metz by motor movement. Eighty-five trucks were attached to the regiment for transportation.

The regiment conducted a training schedule during this period along with rehabilitation. The schedule included an hour's march, close order drill and classes.

# 23 January 1945

CT 137 jumped from the III Corps of the 3rd Army to the XV Corps of the 7th Army on January 23 as the regiment moved by motor from Fort Moselle, Metz to an area in the vicinity of Chateau Salins. The status of the regiment was Corps reserve. The Combat Team moved in a southeasterly direction through the extremely cold and windy weather.

The 137th Infantry moved into its assembly area by 1530. 2nd Bn was located in Grousisville. The regiment was to await further orders from XV Corps Headquarters.

# 24 January 1945

The 137th Infantry moved by motor from its assembly area in the vicinity of Chateau Salins to an area in the vicinity of Montbronn, and relieved the 398th Infantry of the 100th Division in its defensive positions during the night. The 2nd Bn moved up into Lemberg. The regiment received a number of reinforcements today.

# 25 January 1945

On January 25 the 137th Infantry was holding the positions it had taken over from the 398th Infantry during the early morning. The 2nd Bn was on the left, its CP in Lemberg, and its troops holding ground on the outskirts of the town and to the south.

The 2nd Bn completed its relief by 0230 and received five rounds of 120mm mortar fire at 0845 and several casualties were suffered. At 1335, three rounds of artillery coming from the rear killed three men.

# 26 January 1945

The 137th Infantry continued to hold its defensive positions vacated by the 398th Infantry and sporadic fire was received by the battalions throughout the day, although there was no heavy action.

All battalions were ordered to send out reconnaissance patrols today and the night of January 26–27.

# 27 January 1945

The snow continued to fall throughout the day as the 137th Infantry maintained its defensive positions on January 27, holding and improving them.

Patrols reported enemy action throughout the front of the regiment's sector. The battalions were rotating their companies, with two outfits on the line, and the third rifle company in reserve.

# 28 January 1945

On January 28, the 137th Infantry continued to hold and improve its positions in its sector of defense. Patrolling activity was conducted.

# 29 January 1945

The 137th Infantry was relieved of its sector by the 398th Infantry on January 29 and the regiment moved by motor to a rear assembly area. The 2nd Bn was relieved by 2115.

The 2nd Battalion moved to Berg. The regiment was billeted in the town for the night prior to moving out in the morning by train and motor for Holland.

# 30 January 1945

January 30, the 137th Infantry began its movement to Holland. The 137th's organic transportation moved out on its two day journey. The remainder of the regiment moved by truck from the assembly area to Reding and boarded trains for a three day move to Holland.

# 31 January 1945

The 137th Infantry continued on its move up into Holland, on January 31. Troops moving by rail traveled through Luneville, Nancy, Toul, Verdun, Sedan, Mezieres, Namur, Liege and stopped at Vise on February 1, during the three day move by train.

The regiment was now assigned to the Ninth Army along with the 35th Division.

Casualties for the month of January were: 4 officers and 54 EM killed in action, 2 officers and 220 EM wounded in action, and 2 officers and 46 EM missing in action. 23 prisoners passed through the 137th Infantry PW cage during the month.

Report After Action Against Enemy
Hq 137th Inf 1 Feb 45

For the Commanding Officer:

LLOYD D. FRIEDMAN
Capt., Infantry
Adjutant

1 Incl:
   1 Unit Journal
      with supporting
      papers.

- 10 -

S E C R E T

S E C R E T

HEADQUARTERS 137TH INFANTRY
APO 35          U S ARMY

Auth: CG 35th Inf Div
Initials _____
Date 18 Mar 1945
   1 March 1945

176

For the Commanding Officer:

LLOYD D. FRIEDMAN
Capt., Infantry
Adjutant

HEADQUARTERS 137TH INFANTRY
APO 35      U S ARMY
SUBJECT: Report After Action Against Enemy
TO      : The Adjutant General
        Washington 25, D.C.

1. In compliance with the provisions of Par 10 03, AR 345-105, submitted below is report after action against enemy for the 137th Infantry covering the period 1–28 February 1945.

# 1 February 1945

Troops of the 137th Infantry, following their three day train ride from Southern France, arrived in Vise, Belgium on the morning of February 1, and moved by motor to the regiment's assembly area in the vicinity of Banholt, Holland.

The regiment's new assembly area was located north of Liege and east of the Netherlands city of Maastricht. 2nd Bn moved to Scheg.

# 2–3 February 1945

The 137th Infantry Regiment remained in its assembly area February 2 and 3 as the 35th Division remained in XVI Corps reserve.

# 4 February 1945

The 35th Division was ordered to relieve elements of the British 52nd Infantry Division of the 2nd Army in defensive positions inside Germany on February 5. The 137th Infantry was to move by motor from its assembly area in Holland to the sector held by the 156th Brigade. The regiment was to occupy and defend the same defensive positions held by the British infantry.

# 5 February 1945

The 137th Infantry entered Germany for a second time, when on February 5 the regiment relieved the 156th Brigade of the British 52nd Division in its defensive positions, west of the Roer River.

In the central sector the 2nd Bn relieved the 6th Camerions, as its troops moved into positions in Kirchoven and Lieck.

## 6 February 1945

On February 6, the 137th Infantry was holding its defensive positions taken over from the 156th Infantry, 52nd British Division.

A Co A patrol, conducting a reconnaissance to the front, was pinned down by enemy fire coming from a nearby building. Reinforcements were sent out to contact the patrol, but failed to locate the Co A men. It was believed that the patrol of one officer and four EM were captured by the enemy.

The roads in the regimental sector were in poor condition due to mud and rain, and a number of roads were impassable to vehicles.

## 7 February 1945

Foot patrols were conducted again today during daylight between the front line troops and the Roer River. There was increased flare activity over the front during the night.

## 8–9–10 February 1945

On February 8 the 137th Infantry was to be relieved of its sector by the 8th Armored Division, but the relief was postponed and the regiment continued to hold and defend its positions. Patrolling went on as usual but the regiment was ordered not to cross any water barriers.

## 11 February 1945

The enemy destruction of the mighty Schwammenauel Dam today sent tons of water flooding down upon the Roer Valley, causing the Roer River to rise as much as seven feet. In the 137th area, it overflowed its banks and flooded large areas. Two 12 round barrages of heavy artillery hit the 2nd Bn at 1810.

## 12 February 1945

The 137th Infantry and the enemy watched each other across the enemy-created flood of the Roer River as the regiment maintained its defensive positions.

Major General Baade, 35th Division Commander, directed that all troops be alerted to the fact that the enemy might conduct raids into the regiment's lines up to and including company strength.

## 13 February 1945

A 2nd Bn patrol, conducting a reconnaissance to the Roer River, went through the woods south of Haag and entered the first building of the German town when it was confronted by a 20 man enemy patrol. After a short fire fight, during which the enemy attempted to outflank the 137th men, the 2nd Bn patrol withdrew safely back into the woods.

# 14 February 1945

At 1535 when the 2nd Bn fired on a 16-man enemy patrol in the vicinity of Haag the enemy withdrew to buildings north of Haag.

# February 1945

The sun was shining and the weather turned warmer on February 15 as the 137th Infantry continued to hold and defend its positions. Enemy artillery fire was light, as in the past few days.

# 16–17–18 February 1945

Co K killed two of their own men at 0515 when they were challenged and failed to halt. At 1030 on February 18, an enemy patrol followed a Co E patrol which was returning to its lines. The enemy fled when the 137th men fired on them.

# 19–20–21 February 1945

From February 19 to 21, the 137th Infantry continued the defense of its sector west of the Roer River, and also conducted assault boat training in a rear area. During the night there was much flare activity reported by all units along the front.

The 2nd and 3rd Bns each received light artillery fire on February 20. The church steeple in Kirchoven was hit by three rounds at 1257.

A British Lancaster bomber crashed 1,000 yards north of Heinsberg and 200 yards in front of 2nd Bn positions at 0150 on February 21. A 2nd Bn patrol found the plane to be free of personnel but removed the navigational equipment and maps which it discovered in the wreck.

At 0842 all companies were alerted when 25 to 30 enemy were observed crossing the Roer River in boats. Three additional boat loads of from six to eight men each, crossed to the western shore of the river at 0900. Mortars were brought forward to engage the enemy and any others attempting to cross the river. The enemy failed to make a thrust at any position of the 137th.

# 22–23 February 1945

The 137th Infantry was relieved of its sector at 2307, February 22, by the 314th Infantry of the 79th Division, and then moved back out of Germany into an assembly area in Holland and passed into 35th Division reserve. The 2nd Bn's relief was completed at 2305. At 1900 the order was issued to sew on all 35th Division patches and paint bumper markings on all vehicles at once, since the veil of secrecy was lifted from the Division.

## 24 February 1945

The 137th Infantry remained in division reserve in its assembly area in Holland and conducted reconnaissance for possible commitment into any sector of the division.

## 25 February 1945

The 137th Infantry remained in 35th Division reserve until the evening of February 25 and then moved by motor to cross the Roer River and attack in the sector assigned to it, adjacent to the 84th Infantry Division.

The regiment was to cross the Roer River to Korrenzig, then move by foot to Doveren, then on to the Line of Departure and attack at 0600 February 26.

## 26 February 1945

The 137th Infantry crossed the Roer River by motor under cover of darkness and attacked at 0630 against the stiff enemy resistance encountered during the day.

The 2nd Bn attacked in a column of companies. The advance was met by heavy mortar, artillery and SP fire. Co F moved through the woods east of Huckelhoven under mortar fire, while Co E with a platoon of tanks followed, proceeding along the road to the right of the woods. The battalion pulled up at the stream bed near the edge of the woods, dug in, and blazed away at the enemy confronting it.

## 27 February 1945

Continuing the attack a second day, the 137th Infantry shoved ahead on February 27 and pitched the enemy out of Gerderath, the woods southwest of Gerderath, Fronderath, Gerderhahn, and Almyhl. The regiment received exceptional work from Co B, 784th Tank Bn, a negro unit which was attached to the 137th for the operation.

The 2nd Bn launched its attack from Gladbach at 0600 with the 784th tanks and tank destroyers from the 654th Bn. The Bn fanned out, went through the woods southwest of Gerderath, moved across the stream and cleaned out a patch of woods 500 yards wide, below Myhl. The work of Co B, 784th Tk Bn, had been exceptional all day, and the negro tankers supported the regiment in an excellent manner all day.

# 28 February 1945

February 28, the 137th infantrymen trudged ahead working through the Birgeler Woods and seizing the towns of Wildenrath, Rodge, Arsbeck and Station-Vlodrop. The enemy offered slight resistance of small arms, automatic weapons, and SP gun fire on leading elements of the 137th during the day's operations.

A 407th Group, XVI Corps observation plane was shot down over the 1st Bn area and the pilot was slightly wounded and treated by 137th medical aid men.

The regiment had advanced 6,000 meters during the day, clearing road blocks and flushing cellars in the towns passed through.

The battle casualties for the month of February were 2 officers and 46 enlisted men.

Report After Action Against Enemy
Hq 137th Inf 1 March 45

Incl:
Journal and supporting papers

W. S. MURRAY
Colonel, Infantry
Commanding

Incl:
Journal and supporting papers

W. S. MURRAY
Colonel, Infantry
Commanding

Auth: CG 35th Inf Div
Initials *R.G.C.*
Date *14 apr 45*
1 April 1945

HEADQUARTERS 137TH INFANTRY
APO 35        U S ARMY

# HEADQUARTERS 137TH INFANTRY
## APO 35        U S ARMY

SUBJECT:  Report After Action Against Enemy
To        :  The Adjutant General
              Washington 25, D.C.

1. In compliance with the provisions of Par 10 C3, AR 345-105, submitted below is report after action against enemy for the 137th Infantry covering period 1–31 March 1945.

## 1–2 March 1945

March 1 found the 137th Infantry Combat Team continuing its swift attack toward the Rhine River. The 137th's mission was to advance and close into an assembly area near Leuth, Germany, southeast of Venlo, Holland.

## 3–4 March 1945

The 137th Infantry CT departed from its assembly area in the vicinity of Venlo, Holland at 1500, March 3, and moved by foot and motor to an assembly area west of Nieukirk, Germany, where it closed by 1900. The 2nd and 1st Bns left their areas and marched 14 miles through the night prior to jumping off in an attack at 0700, March 4.

The 2nd Bn launched its drive and swiftly secured the town of Rheurdt, southeast of Lintfort. The Bn seized two bridges intact over the Fleuth Landwehr at 1000.

## 5–6 March 1945

After Lintfort had been taken on March 5, Task Force Murray, which included the 8th Armored Division, in a daring night attack captured the city of Rheinberg.

The 8th Armored desired to seize Lintfort by attacking through the 137th's 2nd Bn, a plan which was mutually agreed upon by the respective commanders. The attack began at 0700 with the 8th Armored rolling into the city while the 2nd Bn made a demonstration, then assisted the armor by fire and followed it into the city.

Task Force Murray became effective as of 1600, March 5, and was composed of many units including the 137th Infantry Regiment, the 784th Tk Bn and several others. Its mission was to twist north and take Ossenberg, then move on across the Rhine River with Wesel as its final objective.

The 8th Armored stabbed toward Rheinberg in the afternoon and received a jolting punishment from the enemy in the city. The 2nd and 3rd Bns of the 137th had become motorized when Lintfort was taken and had followed the armor to the outskirts of the city.

A night attack was planned to capture Rheinberg, a plan only a veteran, experienced unit could fulfill. In a daring and shrewd move, the 2nd and 3rd Bns entered Rheinberg at 2012. After dismounting from the trucks, the Bns made contact and worked their way down the main street, the 3rd Bn on one side, the 2nd on the other. After flushing out dark cellars and buildings, Rheinberg was nearly cleaned up by 0300. There were still fire fights until 0600 when the city was mopped up and securely outposted. The negro tankers of the 784th added a touch to the victory by prefacing their entry into the city with a sensational dash through five miles of enemy lines to the Rhine River itself.

For the remainder of the day, the 2nd and 3rd Bns were checked outside of Rheinberg by a blown bridge. The men couldn't move against the heavy enemy fire directed at them across the flat expanses of terrain without the support of tanks, and armor couldn't cross the stream until a bridge was built. The drive continued at 1800 as soon as the bridge was put in, with Ossenberg the next objective. Artillery had pounded Ossenberg day and night so that it might be taken and a stop put to the enemy's retreat across the river above the city.

# 7 March 1945

On March 7th, Task Force Murray was fighting in the outskirts of Ossenberg while absorbing all types of intense enemy fire. The road from Rheinberg to Ossenberg gave the 137th its bitterest opposition encountered during the entire operation and was dubbed "88 Alley." The enemy was determined to hold Ossenberg in order to keep its pocket west of the Rhine River and Wesel.

The 2nd Bn remained in Ossenberg and prepared to attack along the Rhine the following day.

# 8 March 1945

Task Force Murray was hammering away at the southern edge of the enemy pocket north of Ossenberg on March 8. The 2nd Bn went around Ossenberg and edged its way north under violent enemy fire. The 2nd Bn was to move along the highway just west of the Rhine River up to smaller Borth and then advance on to Augenedshorf and continue northeast up the highway to Buderich, on up to Fort Bulcher, then across the Rhine to Budericher and on to Wesel, the final objective of TF Murray.

# 9 March 1945

The 2nd Bn was pinned down by vicious enemy fire from the eastern side of the Rhine River.

# 10 March 1945

On March 19, TF Murray had its boundary changed and after the 137th had smashed ahead and seized Borch and Wallach, it was pinched out by the 134th CT, attacking toward Wesel.

# 11–12 March 1945

On March 11 and 12 the 137th Infantry remained in its positions along the bank of the Rhine River. At 2135 the 137th Infantry was relieved in its zone by the 209th Infantry, Regiment of the 75th Division and prepared to move March 13 to a rear assembly area.

# 13–15 March 1945

When the 35th Division was relieved of its responsibilities along the Rhine River front, the 137th Infantry moved by motor to a rear assembly area in Germany, southeast of Venlo, Holland. The 2nd Bn closed into Lutherheide by 1100.

# 16–22 March 1945

The 35th Infantry Division remained in XVI Corps reserve of the Ninth Army from March 16 to March 22. The 75th Infantry Division was holding the Corps front along the Rhine River.

# 23–25 March 1945

The offensive to win the war in Europe was launched at 2200 hours, March 23, as the Ninth Army, British and Canadian troops, shrouded by a 66 mile long smoke screen, crossed the Rhine River in assault craft of every type. The Ninth Army bridgehead was established 12 miles south of Wesel.

March 25 the 35th Division was alerted to move forward as soon as operational space was provided by the 30th and 79th Divisions, battling east of the Rhine.

## 26 March 1945

The 137th Infantry moved by motor March 26 to a forward Assembly area east of the Rhine River and prepared to attack the next morning between the 30th and 79th Divisions.

The regimental motor column departed from its area and moved through Rheinberg, then crossed the Rhine River south of Mehrum on a pontoon bridge under an umbrella of air protection and proceeded to Dinslaken-Bruch. The 3 Bns moved into an area east of the town.

## 27 March 1945

Leaving the northern Rhine bridgehead south of Wesel, the 137th Infantry Regiment knifed into the northern section of the Ruhr industrial area March 27 against stubborn enemy resistance.

The 2nd Bn with the 784th Tk Bn attacked the right sector, taking Waldhuck and Sterkrade-Nord by 2030. The superhighway was stiffly defended as 2nd Bn troops advanced to a point 1,000 yards west of the Autobahn. The Bn ran into opposition at 0920 as the enemy directed SP and machine gun fire at the men. Co E was confronted by an enemy tank at the same time. It was believed that the enemy was using dummy tanks to draw fire.

Twenty three men of Cos G and H were killed or captured when they unknowingly advanced into enemy territory to establish a CP in a building, were isolated and had no means of possible escape.

The 137th Infantry was encountering severe enemy resistance March 28 as the regiment contacted the Autobahn superhighway, east of Konigshardt.

Today the 35th Division with the 134th Regiment on the left, the 137th Regiment in the center and the 320th Regiment on the right was flanked on the left by the 30th Division and on the right by the 79th Division. The 30th Division was holding down the left flank of the XVI Corps and the Ninth Army, adjacent to the British Second Army.

Prisoners taken by the 137th said they were to defend the superhighway at all costs and were using dug-in positions along the highway.

# 29 March 1945

The 137th Infantry continued attacking throughout the night of March 28–29 and by morning had three companies across the Autobahn highway. When the attack ceased at 1900, the 137th had reached the suburbs of Kol Rheinbaben, Eigen and Bottrop. The 137th ceased the attack at 1900 and was directed to continue at 0700, March 30.

The fact that the 137th had captured 290 German soldiers in its sector during three days fighting, proved that the enemy was determined to hold the ground along the northern Ruhr Valley.

# 30 March 1945

The 1st and 2nd Bns broke away from Kol Rheinbaben and Bottrop on March 30 and made an 8,000 yard advance which took them to the Topeks Objective. The 137th was attacking east just 6,000 yards north of the city of Essen with its Krupp Steel Works. The regiment's boundaries were the Autobahn superhighway on the left and the Rhine-Herne Canal on the right.

The 2nd Bn advanced in its sector, shooting through Eastern Eigen Siebeck and others. The regimental CP moved to Bottrop at 1400 and from Bottrop to Gladbeck at 1900.

# 31 March 1945

The 137th Infantry rolled swiftly east March 31, gaining from 6,000 to 7,000 yards and capturing 100 Nazi soldiers. The 1st and 2nd Bns received scattered artillery fire in the early morning, prior to jumping off for the day.

The 2nd Bn began to move out of Buer Beckhausen at 0710 and advanced past Buer Erle and knifed approximately 1,000 yards into the Kol Ewald Woods.

The battle casualties for the month of March are 12 officers and 227 EM.

W.S. MURRAY
Colonel, Infantry

Incl: Commanding
Journal and supporting papers

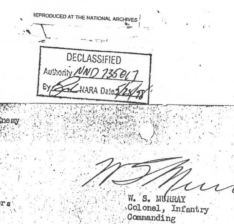

Report After Action Against Enemy
Hq 137th Inf 1 April 45

Incl:
Journal and supporting papers

W. S. MURRAY
Colonel, Infantry
Commanding

- 8 -

### HEADQUARTERS 137TH INFANTRY
### APO 35       U S ARMY

SUBJECT: Report After Action Against Enemy
TO     : The Adjutant General
          Washington 25, D. C.

    1. In compliance with the provisions of Par 10 C3, AR345-105, submitted below is report after action against enemy for the 137th Infantry covering the period 1–30 April 1945.

SECRET

HEADQUARTERS 137TH INFANTRY
APO 35      U S ARMY

SECRET

h: CG 35th Inf Div

Initials R. S. C.

Date 27 May 1945.
      1 May 1945

# 1 April 1945

The 137th Infantry continued its eastward advance between the Autobahn superhighway and the Rhein-Herne Canal in the Ruhr Industrial Area on April 1 and toward the end of the day, swung south into a defensive position along the northern bank of the canal.

The regiment had British flame-throwing tanks attached April 1 from the 1st and 2nd platoons, B Squad, 1st Fife and Forfar Yeomanry.

The 2nd Bn moved into the left sector of the regiment's defensive zone along the canal. The 2nd Bn defended the ground from Rollinhausen south to the canal.

# 2–5 April 1945

April 2 to 5 the 35th Division continued its aggressive defense along the Rhein-Herne Canal, sending contact patrols along the canal and reconnaissance patrols south of the canal.

137th Infantry patrols which crossed the canal, located enemy positions on the outskirts of Herne and along the southern bank of the canal. A majority of the enemy captured by the 137th claimed that the enemy force south of the canal desired to surrender to the Americans, since they realized the Ruhr was surrounded.

# 6–8 April 1945

April 7, while the 79th Division had jumped across the canal at 0300, the 137th Infantry assisted by a fire demonstration. The 1st and 2nd Bns of the 137th remained on the line. The boundary between the 1st and 2nd Bns was the road running from Recklinghausen to the canal.

The 137th prepared to attack in the early morning of April 9, crossing the canal and advancing south.

# 9 April 1945

The 137th Infantry crossed the Rhein-Herne Canal under heavy enemy fire on the morning of April 9, secured a bridgehead north of Herne, broke the crust of the enemy defense south of the canal and advanced against scattered resistance to the railroad tracks running through Herne and Wanne-Eickel.

The 2nd Bn crossed the canal in the 1st Bn zone and advanced to Herne's important rail marshalling yard. The attack ceased for the day at 1930.

# 10 April 1945

The 137th Infantry captured Herne, its rail marshalling yard, a portion of Wanne-Eickel and its rail sidings, along with 18 suburban towns on April 10 after attacking from the railroad tracks in the morning.

The three battalions attacked at 0700 and, with practically no opposition, the 2nd Bn was on its objective by 1136.

Herne, with a population of 66,000, was struck from the north. The 2nd Bn on the left swept through Borsinghasen and Mittelfeld to reach the objective. The final objective for the day was the railroad track running through Gerthe to Hiltrop Dorf.

## 11 April 1945

The 137th Infantry attacked to the south April 11, overrunning over 6 miles of Industrial Germany. The 2nd Bn attacked in the left sector and the 1st Bn in the right.

The 2nd Bn jumped off at 0605 and was on its objective, 800 yards north of the Ruhr River, by 1110.

The 137th Infantry continued to hold its position along the north bank of the Ruhr River, awaiting relief by the 79th Division within 48 hours.

## 12 April 1945

The 137th Infantry continued to hold and defend its position along the north bank of the Ruhr River on April 12 awaiting relief by the 79th Division. Upon being relieved, the regiment was to assemble and form a combat team.

## 13 April 1945

The 137th Infantry was relieved in its position along the Ruhr River on April 13 by the 289th Infantry, 79th Division, and then assembled in the vicinity of Laerfeld. At 0800 the 137th Infantry Combat Team began its motor movement from the Ruhr to join forces with that part of the Ninth Army driving eastward toward the Elbe River.

The motorized column started east on its 220 mile move to the Elbe River. The Combat Team arrived in an assembly area in the vicinity of Everingen at 2100.

## 14 April 1945

On April 14, the 137th Infantry CT moved by motor from its rear assembly area in Everingen, approximately 25 miles northeast to the Elbe River, six miles south of Stendal. The CT departed at 1530 and closed into an area in the vicinity of Luderitz by 2150. The 2nd Bn moved into Bellingen.

Armored spearheads to the east had bypassed numerous enemy pockets in the large woods within the 137th's new area, and the regiment discovered it had entered a weird and fluid situation.

# 15 April 1945

April 15 the 137th Infantry flushed the enemy from the woods throughout its sector and patrolled by both foot and motor to the Elbe River. 476 PWs had passed through the 137th PW cage at the conclusion of the day, but it was believed enemy forces were still scattered about the sector.

# 16 April 1945

April 16 the 137th Infantry consolidated its positions along the west bank of the Elbe River after having initially sent patrols to the river bank. The 2nd Bn on the right had a sector extending south to an inland town, Grieberg.

There was much activity observed on the enemy-held east bank of the river during the day and patrols were sent across the Elbe during the night of April 16–17 to determine strength, disposition and identification of enemy and conditions along the east bank, opposite the 137th's front.

# 17 April 1945

The 137th Infantry remained in its defensive position along the west bank of the Elbe River on April 17. During hours of daylight patrols were sent to the river and during darkness, reconnaissance was conducted along the east bank.

The Co E OP was pushed back approximately at 0130 by an enemy force of 50 troops, but mortar fire checked the enemy thrust. The 2nd and 3rd Bns were under shelling during the early morning.

# 18–20 April 1945

From April 18 to 20, the 137th Infantry Regiment continued the defense of its sector along the west bank of the Elbe River.

April 19 613 German PWs were taken by the 137th. Two crashed enemy aircraft were discovered by the 2nd Bn.

Interest on April 20 was focused on CT Clauswitz, an enemy force of 20 SP guns, 30 half tracks, and American vehicles, along with 800 troops, who had cut south between the British and the Ninth Army. After it penetrated 15 miles of ground behind the Ninth Army troops along the Elbe, it was stopped by the 5th Armored Division.

# 21 April 1945

The 137th Infantry remained in position along the west bank of the Elbe River April 21 patrolling actively along the river bank.

The 2nd Bn established its CP in Buch. Co E occupied positions in Buch. At 1705 four enemy aircraft were observed taking off from an undisclosed airstrip on the east side of the river.

## 24–25 April 1945

The 137th continued the defense along the west bank of the Elbe River within its zone. The 3rd Bn received 100 rounds of enemy artillery within thirty minutes during the morning.

## 24–25 April 1945

Russian units spearheading toward the Elbe River were believed to be nearing the positions of the 35th Division on April 24. The Ninth Army Reconnaissance reported a large number of unidentified vehicles in several groups moving in a northwesterly direction toward the Elbe.

The no fire line for the 137th Infantry was the Elbe River and all units within the regiment were reminded of this. At 2305, Co E observed two green flares, at the time believed to be a signal from the Russians. Two officers of the 2nd Bn crossed the Elbe during the night in an attempt to contact the Russians. After firing flares on the east bank and moving 800 yards inland without success, they returned to the west bank of the river.

The 2nd Bn heard motor movement in Jerichow at 0520 and called for artillery to fire on the town. Throughout April 25, the 2nd Bn observed heavy motor movement north out of Jerichow. There was much activity throughout the day all along the eastern shore of the Elbe opposite the 137th Infantry positions.

## 26 April 1945

At 0100, April 26, the 2nd Bn Commander, two members of his staff, a Co G officer and a mess sergeant set out on a mission which, if at all possible, was to contact the Russians. When they reached the west bank of the river they began firing green flares in an effort to attract the Russians. One of the flares lit up a barge floating on the eastern bank, on which enemy soldiers were loading ammunition. Two members of the patrol fired on the enemy, and the fire was returned by the enemy, forcing the 2nd Bn patrol to make a strategic withdrawal.

The German civilians on the east side of the river were very aware of the fact that Russians were approaching them. 60 civilians came across the Elbe in the 3rd Bn sector. Co F brought two medical corp officers across to the 2nd Bn who wished to surrender their field hospital of 356 patients and 25 nurses if it could be evacuated across the river to the west side. Lt. Col George O'Connell, the 2nd Bn Commander, on approval by Col William Murray, the 137th Commander, made a deal with the two officers, that only if they rounded up all the American PWs in their area and brought them down to the river bank, would they be allowed to bring the hospital across the river.

They brought 15 Americans and 33 other Allied PWs to the river to meet a 2nd Bn patrol. 14 enemy soldiers also surrendered at that time, and were used to man oars on the boats which ferried the hospital personnel across the river. The hospital was moved to Tangermunde.

The 137th Infantry was relieved of its positions along the river bank at 1855 by elements of the 102nd Division. The regiment then made preparations for a motor movement to the Hanover area where it was to occupy and administer military government in its own particular area.

## 27 April 1945

The 137th Infantry completed a 120 mile motor movement from the Elbe River to the vicinity of Munder south of Hanover on April 27. The regiment was to occupy and govern the area within its zone.

The 2nd Bn moved into Hamelin, the town involved in the tale of the Pied Piper. The entire 35th Division was in the Hanover governing and occupying sector.

## 28–30 April 1945

From April 28 to 30, the 137th Infantry continued to occupy and govern its sector.

The battle casualties for the month of April are as follows: 2 officers and 49 EM.

W. S. MURRAY
Colonel, Infantry

Incl: Commanding
Journal and supporting papers

Report After Action Against Enemy
Hq 137th Inf., 1 May 45

Incls:
Journal and supporting papers

W. S. MURRAY
Colonel, Infantry
Commanding

# APPENDIX II:
## SOUVENIRS

As a youngster in the early 1930s I was fascinated by stories of World War I. It seemed an extremely interesting and exciting time to have lived. Movies of that war made it seem all the more dramatic. Anything connected with World War I immediately caught my interest. It was like taking an emotional trip back in time.

I immediately recognized the even greater historical significance of World War II. It almost felt like living in a history book. It was within that frame of reference that I could look forward to the coming peace when the public would look back at the war as one of the most important historical events of all time.

It was with the above in mind that I started picking up souvenirs that might stir up an emotional response in people with an interest in WWII. There were times when this activity actually deflected my attention away from the unspeakable horrors all around me. The photography in the preceding pages had a similar effect.

Someday, I thought, these tools of death might help satisfy the curiosity of those who weren't there. And so I picked up these items on the battlefield where they were a practically invisible part of the landscape to the soldiers who were primarily interested in survival. Though my interest in these mementoes continues, it sometimes clashes with my feelings about their ultimate death-dealing purpose.

The following pages show some of these tools of war that I sent or carried home.

**The G.I. hand grenade after you pull the pin.**

You pull the ring that you see at the right of the photo. Out comes the cotter pin that keeps the handle in place. Now you are holding the handle in place with your hand. As you throw it, the handle flies off and a firing pin strikes a fuse with a "pop." Five seconds later it explodes, sending pieces in every direction, some of which you see above.

Returning from an outpost at night, we were challenged by a recent replacement. He was supposed to call out a challenge word to which we would reply with a countersign word. He never gave us the challenge word. He merely yelled "Halt!" The next thing we knew we heard the familiar "pop." We needed only two out of the five seconds to hit the dirt. Protected by masonry from shell-torn buildings, the shrapnel whined harmlessly over our heads.

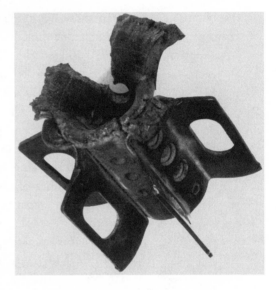

You are looking at what is left of the tail end of a mortar shell after it hit the target. On the outside are four metal fins which stabilize it in flight. The fins are attached to a steel cylinder with holes. Inside the cylinder was a propulsion charge which sent the shell on its way. On landing it exploded and sent jagged pieces of steel in all directions.

As you can see the steel is over ⅛" thick. Imagine what force it took to tear this thick steel apart like it was paper. The flesh of the human body offers very little resistance to these sharp-edged pieces of steel traveling faster than a bullet.

**A mortar shell after it explodes.**

Added to the devilish nature of this weapon, it offers practically no warning of its approach. The standard artillery shell creates a whine that increases in pitch as it approaches. The mortar shell creates barely an audible whisper.

On the following page to the right is the standard cartridge of the U.S. Army in WWII. Its caliber is commonly referred to as 30-06. The 30 stands for the 0.30 inches of its bullet's diameter. The 06 stands for the year 1906 when it was adopted. With this cartridge in the M-1 rifle, I could hit anything I could see. It was still very deadly at 600 yards. The problem was I couldn't tell an American from a German at that distance. This powerful cartridge had a substantial recoil which required skillful training to ignore.

The eight cartridges in the clip could be fired as fast as you could pull the trigger. The rifle's accuracy was first rate. Mostly I fired it into windows and trees where there was a possibility of a hidden enemy. The cartridge at the top of the page was for a rifle that was standard in the German Army in both WWI and WWII. This rifle is known as the Mauser Model 98. Although exceptionally well made, it had a bolt action which had to be operated for every shot. This was very fortunate for

195

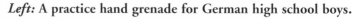

***Above:*** **What they shot at us...** ***Right:*** **What we shot at them...**

me because the German shooting at me running into Malau-court was able to get off only one shot. From the loudness of the crack, I judged the bullet passed my head within six inches, setting my ears ringing.

Note that the American cartridge is a shiny raw brass. The German cartridge is painted a dark green. The Germans couldn't get enough brass so they used steel instead. The raw steel, being very hard, could damage the chamber of the rifle. By giving the cartridge a thin coat of paint they solved the problem.

At left is a practice hand grenade I found in a German high school gym. Made for German high school boys, it is the same size, shape and heft as the real thing, which I got to use in a replacement depot on the way to the front. They were using captured German material to make us familiar with the enemy's equipment. We called it a "potato masher." I did have an opportunity to use the real thing. At the base of the handle there is a cap which you unscrew. Inside there is a little bead attached to a string. After the string is pulled there is an eight second delay before it explodes.

On a night patrol out in front of Gremercey Forest, two of these potato mashers were thrown at us. We were in a ditch so the shrapnel flew harmlessly over our heads. While none of us were hurt, the exploding grenades were a significant influence in our decision to go back.

A practice hand grenade for high school boys! What does

***Left:*** **A practice hand grenade for German high school boys.**

that say about Hitler's Germany? I saw a militaristic state with conquest as the ultimate goal.

This practice grenade is made of wood with nothing but a heavy steel cylinder fitted over one end. I drilled a hole in the other end and hung it over my workbench next to a hammer. I used it in place of the regular hammer when its round shape made it more appropriate for the job at hand.

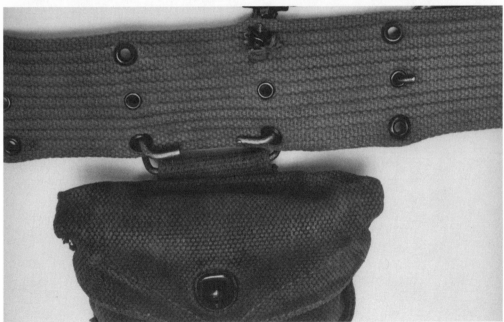

**The G.I. belt I wore in combat.**

The G. I. belt I wore in combat is shown on the previous page.

My belt was supporting a great deal of heavy equipment around my waist. Ordinarily this problem was solved by straps coming over my shoulders from a knapsack on my back. However, running across a field and hopping over fences while being shot at made the knapsack a luxury I could not afford. What to do?

I came across some military suspenders some German soldier had discarded on the road. In attempting to adapt them to my belt, I could not get the snap hooks to go through the eyelets in my belt. Eventually I got the hooks to go through part of the way and then had to bend the hooks with a rock. The picture at the top shows the result more clearly. It served the purpose.

# INDEX

199